The Hummingbird Principle

The Hummingbird Principle

Seven Lenses for Becoming More Human

Chris Burke & Anne de Wild

White River Press
Amherst, Massachusetts

First published 2024 by White River Press
Amherst, Massachusetts • whiteriverpress.com

ISBN: 979-8-88545-015-7 (hardcover)
         979-8-88545-013-3 (paperback)
         979-8-88545-018-8 (ebook)

Book and cover design by Chris Burke and Lufkin Graphic Designs
Norwich, Vermont • www.LufkinGraphics.com

Library of Congress Cataloging-in-Publication Data

Names: Burke, Christopher (Psychologist) | Wild, Anne de, 1971-
    author.
Title: The hummingbird principle : seven lenses for becoming more human /
    Chris Burke and Anne de Wild.
Description: Amherst, Massachusetts : White River Press, [2024]
Identifiers: LCCN 2024003737 | ISBN 9798885450157 (hardcover)
ISBN 9798885450133 (paperback)
Subjects: LCSH: Psychology--Philosophy. | Anthroposophy. | Mythology.
Classification: LCC BF38 .B857 2024 | DDC 150.1--dc23/eng/20240325
LC record available at https://lccn.loc.gov/2024003737

Contents

Introduction

Look around. What do you see in the world around you? The chances are good that you see reasons to despair—war, poverty, fear and hatred of those who are different, a polarized and divisive political discourse, the rejection of long-held traditions and social conventions. Perhaps closer to home you feel the stress of modern life—sustaining a career, managing a family, keeping yourself and others healthy and safe. Maybe you are also dealing with unemployment, addiction, ailing elders, loneliness, marital troubles, alienation. The world seems to be on fire, with the basic foundations of social life faltering.

Now look inside yourself. What do you see? What can you see? What do you really know about yourself? Try to see yourself standing apart from the groups you belong to and the roles you play. Try to peer through the fog of defenses that you've built up to protect yourself from being rejected or hurt or criticized or dehumanized. Can you catch a glimpse of that tiny and vulnerable and striving and wonderfully beautiful core that you might call "I"? When was the last time you quieted down the inner and outer chatter enough to ponder such questions?

This book begins with a simple premise: The social strife we see in the world has roots in our own alienation from ourselves. As we lose hold of who we are as individuals, we connect ourselves to groups that help us feel that we are valuable and that the world is coherent and meaningful. When these groups are threatened, we dig in our heels and take on an "us vs. them" mindset, which further erodes the social fabric. For instance, individuals may dread seeing their relatives at holidays because of differences in political opinions. Or maybe a neighborhood loses its sense of community because it struggles to welcome newcomers who look or think or pray differently. When family and community break down, structures of authority—police, the military, a strong centralized government, the legal system—become more important because we've also lost the capacity to manage ourselves. And so we despair: "The problems are so big, what can I do?"

Anthroposophy and Human Biography

The goal of this book is to provide a framework for reconnecting with ourselves in order to reconnect in a healthy way with our loved ones and the broader world around us. It is based on an approach known as biography work, which has its roots in the spiritual philosophy known as anthroposophy, first described by Rudolf Steiner around the turn of the twentieth century. The word anthroposophy comes from the Greek words "ánthropos" (human being) and "sophía" (wisdom).

Steiner describes anthroposophy as "a path of knowledge to guide the Spiritual in the human being to the Spiritual in the universe"[1] and "the consciousness of one's humanity."[2] Steiner's work, which is comprised of twenty-eight books and over six thousand lectures, reflects his dedication to this path of knowledge and his commitment to share it with others. His works can be broadly classified as philosophical works that articulate the philosophical grounding of anthroposophy; practical works that describe the path of spiritual development and offer guidance for anyone to follow that path; and results of spiritual investigation, in which Steiner applies the knowledge he accessed to such diverse fields as education, agriculture, and social reform. These insights paved the way for Waldorf education, biodynamic agriculture, and the threefold social order—ideas that are experiencing a surge of interest a century later.

To Steiner, the human being is intimately connected to the Earth, such that nature only reaches its full potential through the interest and activity of the human being: "Human beings! Look around you at the world; the world is full of riddles, full of mystery. . . . We can say: All the riddles of the world are solved in the human being—again in the very widest sense. The human beings themselves moving as living beings through the world—they are the solution of the world-riddle!"[3] To say that the human being is the solution to the mysteries of the world indicates, however, that this solution cannot be fixed—it is as dynamic as human beings are growing and developing, and as varied as human beings are from one another.[4]

In Steiner's picture, the essential role of the human being necessitates that knowledge of the world, including knowledge of human beings, is inherently subjective—that is, what is observed and understood depends on the vantage point of the observer. Rather than suggesting an "anything goes" approach to truth, however, Steiner advocates for a truth that can only be seen when every vantage point is grasped:

> This is how people talk: "That is my standpoint." Everyone has a standpoint—as if the standpoint matters! The standpoint in spiritual life is just as fleeting as it is in the physical. Yesterday I stood in Dornach [Switzerland], today I am standing here [Stuttgart, Germany]. These are two different standpoints in physical life. What matters is that people should have a sound will and a sound heart so that they can look at the world from every standpoint. But people today do not want what they can glean from different standpoints; the egoistic assertion of their own particular standpoint is more important to them. But thus individuals shut themselves off in the most rigorous way from their fellow-humans. If somebody says something, the other person does not really enter into it, for they have their own standpoint. But people do not get any nearer to each other by such means. We can only come nearer to each other when we know how to place our different standpoints in a world that is common to us all. But this world is simply not there today. Only in the spirit is there a world that is common to all—and the spirit is lacking.[5]

To look at something from many different angles connects individuals to one another and lets them grow in their ability to understand one another and come together in the spirit.

Steiner also provided a picture of the continuous process of human development over time. Humanity as a whole is going through a series of developmental stages—a gradual process of growth, blossoming, regeneration, and decline that is reflected in the life cycle of individual human beings. In other words, just as an individual is born as an infant and grows through childhood into adulthood and old age, so too is humanity as a whole. This relationship of macro to micro means that studying how humanity has developed over the millennia can shed light on how development unfolds over the life span of an individual. It also means that we can build a picture of the richness of the human being as we form a clearer picture of our own life story—our *biography*.

To some extent, each person's biography is a recapitulation of the archetypal human being. That is, we are all part of the same human story, and there can be great value in learning that a difficult experience that you think is *your* experience is one that is common at a particular stage of life. Building an image of this archetype can serve as a baseline against which you can judge your own experiences, or those of others. For instance, parenting books often provide the typical timing of various developmental milestones—both positive and challenging—to help parents make sense of their children's growing capabilities.

That said, from the moment of birth—even before birth—we are also one of a kind. We are born into different families in different locations at different points in time with different family structures, proclivities, physical and psychological limitations, and predispositions. Even identical twins—born at essentially the same time and place and raised in the same environment—develop distinct stories over time.

How can we make sense of these differences? The circumstances into which individuals are born are perhaps the most obvious source of differences. The existential philosopher Martin Heidegger used the term *thrown-ness*[6] to describe the fact that we are thrown into certain circumstances in life, and that these factors, which fall completely outside of our control, can have a big impact on our trajectory throughout life (e.g., whether we are surrounded by safety, opportunity, and abundance during childhood, or instability, poverty, and abuse). Aside from these "givens," we inhabit different social spheres—parents, grandparents, neighbors, teachers, friends—that grow increasingly individualized over time. We also have different experiences, some of which come through our own choice or striving, and others that come to meet us whether we want them or not. Finally, there seems to be something that works through us. It's the spark of enthusiasm for accounting or botany or customer relations that your friends don't catch. Or the feeling of finding your soulmate and wondering how nobody else before you could have seen how totally perfect this person is. Or your quirky sense of humor. You can't point to where these inclinations come from, but you know with certainty that they are integral to the person you are.

Of course, life also brings each of us some amount of adversity, pain, and suffering. Some of us may try to reject or deny these experiences as part of our biographies, while others may internalize them and become stunted by them. We may construct defenses to avoid thinking about them or to prevent future problems. These defenses could include a whole host of behaviors, from bullying to social withdrawal to substance abuse. While we may often want to forget about the painful experiences of our lives, from an anthroposophical perspective, all of our experiences—pleasant and unpleasant—form a coherent whole that make the biography comprehensible.

Think of the last time you read a biography of a public figure. Imagine how different the story would have been if it only included the person's successes. For many, such a change would make the book not worth reading—like a film with no conflict or tension. In this context, we have an implicit recognition of the value of the difficulties and setbacks. Such obstacles can provide a necessary course correction, point out an error in strategy or planning, or build character traits that will be needed down the road. And we can see the necessity of these experiences for the story without blaming the person for their misfortunes and without exonerating individuals who may have caused the person's suffering.

Applying the same detached, objective perspective to our own biographies is not so easy. Why? Well, one reason is that our stories are still in progress. We can't see clearly where we will ultimately end up and what we will have accomplished, so it's hard to see the difficult experiences as instrumental. Another reason has to do with those defenses just mentioned: You wanted that promotion so badly; you were sure that you were meant to be with the partner who dumped you; no good could possibly come from being displaced by a natural disaster or war.

How can you create enough distance from the events of your life to see their interdependence, their unity? Biography work is one approach. Biography work is a dedicated practice of self-discovery, in which individuals slowly construct a picture of the human being and of themselves as unique human beings. In biography work, we loosen up and gather past experiences to find the patterns and threads, the helpers and the turning points that weave together to form our life story. Biography work begins by simply bringing your attention to the events in your life without overlaying any judgments about them. As you do so, you can invite a sense of curiosity and wonder: "I wonder why that didn't turn out how I expected"; "I wonder if those events were related in some way"; "I wonder why *that* memory came to mind." The goal is not to force a particular story to fit the experiences, but rather to embrace the unknowing and allow insights to emerge when the time is right. Like the poet Rainer Maria Rilke said so eloquently, we have to learn "to be patient towards all that is unsolved in [our] heart[s] and try to love the questions themselves."[7]

Our way of working stems from our training in Biography and Social Art. While many biography activities can be worked through alone, we find that the value added by working with others is immense. Not only does hearing the stories of others help to highlight your own uniqueness and what it means to be human, but there is also a kind of alchemical magic in simply being listened to. Somehow just being able to shine your story into the nonjudgmental mirror of another person allows you to see yourself with greater clarity. When working with groups in person or online, we also use creative activities to bring different kinds of memories into focus for participants. For instance, we might invite participants to create a sketch or poem related to a past experience, and then share the results of the reflection with others. To capture something of this way of working in a book, we have included prompts throughout the chapters that call your attention to moments in your biography.

We place a lot of emphasis on the quality of listening that individuals bring to this work. In everyday interactions, people often fail to really hear what others are saying. They have other things on their minds. They have something *they* want to say, and they are looking for a space to add their two cents. They are already planning a response to what the speaker is saying. Or they are listening while continuing to engage in some other task. This way of listening does not make a speaker feel heard, and it limits what the listener themselves might have gained from the conversation. Alternatively, we suggest practicing open and receptive listening. In this form of listening, the speaker has your warm, undivided attention, and you are simply receiving what they are offering. You are not preparing a response because you are not going to respond. Rather, you open up a space between yourself and the speaker and invite them to fill it with the story that wants to come. You simply take their words into your heart and allow them to silently reflect back to the speaker without interruption or confirmation—as if your mere presence allows them to hear an echo of their story, which can deepen their learning. And while you are not planning to respond to what is being shared with you, do not be surprised if there is a little gift waiting for you at the end—a piece of *your* story that the stranger in front of you has been carrying all these years, just waiting for this sacred moment to return it to you.

The Hummingbird Principle

Our work is inspired by a wonderful Indigenous story from South America, retold by Michael Nicoll Yahgulanaas in the book *The Little Hummingbird*. The story tells of a great forest fire that has all the animals frightened. They are disoriented, paralyzed with fear, and hopeless as the fire rages on. The one exception is a little hummingbird who is darting back and forth from the stream to the fire, each time picking up a single drop of water to quench the blaze. When the other animals finally stop the hummingbird and ask what she is doing, the hummingbird simply replies, "I'm doing everything I can," and continues her work.[8]

There is so much wisdom contained in this story. First, big problems call for collective solutions. You could say that the hummingbird's efforts were futile because of her tiny size and the trivial effect of a single drop of water. But what if all the animals did something? With their collective effort, perhaps they could contain the fire. Everyone is capable of doing something, and if everyone did something maybe these huge problems would not seem so intractable. After all, the problems got so huge in the first place because of the actions and inactions of individuals that compounded over time. And that brings us to the second piece of wisdom: fear and hopelessness can be paralyzing, and it takes courage and resoluteness to act in taxing or dangerous situations. Courage and resoluteness emerge from having a clear sense of purpose: "This is what I must do." Once this state of clarity is reached, action can simply flow out.

Third, and perhaps most importantly for this book, the hummingbird chose to do what she is uniquely suited to do. She has speed, the ability to carry water, and the safety of the air. No other creature in the forest could do what the hummingbird could do. The hummingbird was also aware of her limits. She might have tried to carry two or three drops at a time, but that might have been too much. Stretching beyond her limits might have caused fatigue, error, or even danger. The hummingbird knew herself well enough to know exactly what she was capable of in that moment, and she could see the situation clearly enough to initiate action and persevere in the face of difficulty.

The little hummingbird's approach represents the essence of what we will call *The Hummingbird Principle*. In the simplest terms, the hummingbird principle means being able to see clearly what you can do in a given situation, and then doing it. To do so, you need a realistic assessment of the situation—the issues at hand, the barriers or challenges, and the resources available—as well as a realistic assessment of what you can bring—your talents and abilities, your weaknesses, and situational constraints. Having this clear view of yourself and the situation can also help you appreciate the assets that others bring to the situation and to engage them effectively.

An important part of the hummingbird principle is letting go of preconceptions and expectations. There is no "should" or "ought to" in the hummingbird principle. Action flows from the inner impulse to act based on your assessment of the situation. In any given situation, you can be aware of both your unique talents and more general actions that are within your power, and then choose the course that best meets the demands of the situation. You need not be bound to only acting on your unique talents—that would be another "should" that constrains rather than frees you in the situation. In a different situation, the hummingbird would not continue carrying drops of water just because she is good at it—she would take a fresh look to see how best to get involved. Likewise, you may have a lovely voice, but if the house next door is on fire, it is best to call the fire department rather than to sing a song about it.

Rudolf Steiner uses the term "moral intuition" to describe the capacity for acting out of oneself:

> The action is therefore neither a stereotyped one which merely follows certain rules, nor is it one which we automatically perform in response to an external impulse, but it is an action determined purely and simply by its own ideal content. Such an action presupposes the capacity for moral intuitions . . . [Philosopher Immanuel] Kant's principle of morality—act so that the basis of your action may be valid for all human beings—is the exact opposite of ours. His principle means death to all individual impulses of action. For me, the standard can never be the way all people would act, but rather what, for me, is to be done in each individual case.[9]

Part of the challenge of the time we live in and the deeply entrenched "camps" on any social issue is to develop this sense of moral intuition that brings together our individual perceptions of situations that confront us with a clear view of ourselves to produce an inner impulse to action.

To make these ideas more concrete, we can take an example from the daily news, such as a racially or religiously motivated act of violence occurring in another state. Learning about such an event, you may feel compelled to drop everything, jump on an airplane, and confront the situation directly. While that may sometimes be the best course of action, it is more likely there is something you can do where you live and work that leverages your unique skills to greater effect. Who are the people around you who might be affected by the situation? How can you reach out to them to see how they are doing? Are there ways your skills and abilities can be used to reduce the likelihood that such events can happen in the future, even if only a minor decrease? Are there practical things that those who have been affected are asking for that you can contribute, such as donating blood or food?

Acting out of the hummingbird principle in a given situation requires being prepared and ready to act, and much of this preparation involves developing a realistic understanding of your own abilities and limitations. This is where biography work comes in: biography work is a set of tools for developing a realistic picture of your strengths and weaknesses and for seeing them as a unity that makes your life story comprehensible. Through biography work, you can gain an appreciation that your abilities and limitations are not fixed, but are constantly in flux. Through life experiences, you have been able to cultivate certain abilities—perhaps out of necessity—that you may need to call on in the future. You may also see abilities that are waning as you grow older; learning to accept those changes is one key to remaining effective with age. You may also see ways in which the world itself is changing that either complement or contrast with your strengths. Finally, you may come to appreciate that different stages of life are associated with different ways of orienting to the self and the world, and that those different orientations can be a real asset when trying to tackle complex problems collectively. With this clearer view of yourself, your sight can widen to see the gifts that those around you bring, and to recognize that those gifts were cultivated through life paths that held challenges and opportunities different from your own.

Basic Concepts in Biography Work

To properly set up the coming chapters, following are some basic anthroposophical ideas regarding the nature of the human being. First, the human being is comprised of more than simply material "stuff." In fact, there are four essential components of the human being according to anthroposophy—what is referred to as the fourfold human being.[10] At the first level is the *physical body*. The elements that comprise the physical body are not so different from those of the rocks and soil outside, and once a person dies, the physical body gradually returns to that state, following the laws of the material world. So we can say that having a physical body gives us a certain kinship with the mineral world, which we also share with plants and animals.

The fact of our "returning to dust" after death makes it clear that we need something to give us form and maintain it while we are alive. We call this body the *etheric body* or life-body. The etheric body operates according to laws of rhythm and time—respiration, circulation, and growth. All that lives in us as habit and repetition is anchored in the etheric body. The etheric body never gets tired—it always works effortlessly. All living things have an etheric body, but if we only were made of these two levels (physical and etheric), we would be in the realm of plants. They have a body that is in space and a living form that follows rhythm and time.

The next layer is known as the *astral body*. The astral body is the seat of consciousness—the awareness of one's environment and its contingencies. Consciousness allows for sensation, instincts, passions, desires, and other impulses. The quality of the astral body is inner and outer mobility, and the presence of an astral body distinguishes animals and people from plants. That is, while plants have some sensitivity to environmental circumstances, they cannot act on their environments. We can see this in everyday language as well with the coarse label "vegetable" used to describe someone in a comatose state—an implicit acknowledgment that a person who is alive but lacking consciousness has a plant-like quality.

Finally, there is something that distinguishes the human being from other animals—the capacity for self-awareness, which arises through the presence of what is called the *ego* or "*I*" in anthroposophy. That is, we have the ability to step out of our own thoughts, feelings, intentions, and other inner states and reflect on them. We can ask, "How do I feel about this?" or "What do I think is the easiest solution to this situation?" We can enter into dialogue with ourselves and engage faculties of reasoning. Importantly, we can also self-regulate—we can hold ourselves back in the service of important goals. The ego is the core of the person, and it is what makes each person an individual. The term "ego" has developed a negative connotation in modern life. People are often accused of having an "inflated ego" or of being on an "ego trip"—terms that suggest self-centeredness or self-importance. These kinds of phrases indicate an attachment to a lower self, one that is connected to selfish and materialistic ends. The ego in anthroposophy is a higher self that is rooted in the spiritual world and is striving toward higher ends. Rudolf Steiner states:

> [T]he 'I' is at the same time that which gives human beings their independence and their inner freedom, which in the truest sense of the word elevates them. Their dignity is founded in this 'I,' it is the basis of the Divine in humans. . . . [A]bove all, human beings must strive for the strength (if they understand the mission of the world) to make this 'I' more and more inward, more and more divine."[11]

This excerpt points to another uniquely human task of the ego—personal development. Unlike plants and animals, we are responsible for developing our full potential. Human beings are able to say "I am," and can aspire to become more fully human, whereas a dog can't become "doggier." Its dog-ness is given and only needs training to be contorted into the constraints of human culture. Human beings are called to be active in developing their individual talents and potentialities across the lifespan.

So how do these layers combine to create the individual human being? The physical body is the bearer of the archetypal human form. As soon as we see someone, we instantly recognize their humanity— "Aha, that's a human!" And yet we also recognize the ways in which this individual's physicality stands apart from the "standard model." We might notice a long, straight nose, or a broad jaw, or deep-set eyes, and so on. If we meet the parents or grandparents of the individual, we might see some resemblance and understand that the physical body is also the bearer of heredity—the physical traits and predispositions passed down to us from our parents. It connects us to the stream of our ancestors. Some of these physical similarities may be apparent almost from birth and particularly notable during early childhood. Parents may often remark of their young children: "She has your feet" or "He has my father's ears." As the child grows, these features may undergo transformations, and their prominence may subside as the child's unique personality awakens.

The etheric body holds the first seed of our personalities, known as *temperament*. Developmental psychologists have focused on qualities like impulse control and tendency to experience positive and negative emotions as the core dimensions of temperament, and while some of these qualities can be observed very early, they tend to remain somewhat fluid throughout early childhood.[12] The anthroposophical view of temperament focuses on four types—choleric, sanguine, phlegmatic, melancholic—that have a history going back to Hippocrates (c. 460–375 BC) and his theory of humourism. It was Galen of Pergamum (129–c. 200 AD) who introduced the term "temperament," meaning "mixture."

The choleric types are fiery doers, with a lot of power to start things and the determination to push through any obstacles thrown in the way of their goal. They take charge and can compel people to go along with their ideas in order to get things done. Tact and other soft people skills do not come easily to them, and with their aversion to unfinished tasks, they can easily find themselves overcommitted.

The sanguine types are social butterflies—thriving on attention, fun to be around, friendly, and lighthearted. They get excited about things quickly, but they can just as quickly lose interest and move onto the next possibility. Deep contemplation and long-term planning are not their strong suits. They live more in the moment and are likely to be surrounded by unfinished projects.

The phlegmatic types are "go with the flow" kind of people. They are easy-going, agreeable, and slow to become angry or upset with others. They work well under pressure; with their slow, methodical approach, they can work through difficulties without stressing out. The slow pace of the phlegmatic types can sometimes be out of step with those around them, and they can have difficulties making decisions, taking action, and accepting change.

The melancholic types are very conscientious—organized, thoughtful, and following through with plans. Family and a few close friends are very important to them, and loyalty is a top priority. They have high standards for themselves and others, and they can have difficulty forgiving and forgetting. They can appear serious and sullen, with a heightened sensitivity to their own pain and suffering that opens them to a capacity for deep empathy with the pain and suffering of others.

Perhaps one of these descriptions resonates strongly with you. According to anthroposophy, temperament stabilizes in middle childhood and represents the individual's default way of engaging the world. And while most people can find one of these four as a dominant temperament, nobody is a pure type. With some effort, we can begin to see how each of the others can emerge in particular situations. Thus, everyone has their own blend of the four—what we in our work have dubbed *the fifth temperament*—that is completely their own. Keeping this fact in mind can help individuals resist the urge to pigeonhole themselves or others or to reduce someone's behavior to being "such a choleric" or "so phlegmatic." Developing a sensitivity for the *fifth temperament* means remaining open to which facet of temperament is most prominent in a given situation. Then, through working with our own experiences with people who are good listeners or who have a real interest in us, we can gradually strengthen those aspects that show up less often.

Moving to the astral level, things become much more dynamic. The stable part of the person at this level is what we might call personality or character, but research from the field of personality shows that people's behaviors are not as consistent with personality as one might expect. The astral quality allows the individual to respond to the changing demands of the situation. These character dynamics include moods, mindsets, and motives that are influenced by inner and outer states. As with the temperaments, there are certain prototypes at this astral level that blend together differently in different individuals and different situations. (These are the primary focus of the later chapters.)

Finally, the level of the "I" or Self is what's completely unique to the individual. On the surface level, we can develop an appreciation for the fact that every person treads a unique path through life and has a completely distinct history of experiences that has brought them to the present moment. We might broaden this perspective further and say that, as a being who comes from the realm of spirit, this individual path extends farther back to the time before birth. That is, perhaps the "I" brings with it certain tasks and seeks out certain experiences during the lifetime to carry forward certain spiritual objectives. Going a step further to include the possibility of reincarnation and karma, we could say these tasks might be related to previous incarnations—bringing resolution or reconciliation to certain relationships or making amends for past missteps—as well as the more general task of spiritual development. Becoming open to the possibility of such influences on life's path can bring a newfound appreciation for the little experiences of life that can be so influential or the profound impact that certain individuals have had on us.

The Planets as an Organizing Framework

As we have indicated, the focus of this book is on the dynamic qualities of the astral body—sometimes called soul qualities—that respond to the varied demands of the situations we find ourselves in. We will describe seven prototypic moods of the soul and connect them to both the mundane situations of everyday life and to broader areas of social tension or strife that we can observe in the world. These prototypes derive from the qualities attributed to the seven classical "planets"—those celestial bodies in the solar system that are visible to the naked eye. These include the Sun and Moon, as well as the planets Mercury, Venus, Mars, Jupiter, and Saturn. Throughout the ancient world, these bodies were viewed as having powerful influences on people. These qualities can perhaps most readily be seen in the dramatic myths of Greece and Rome, where gods share names with these planets. Much the way fairy tales can be seen as allegories for inner experiences, so can these myths be seen as expressing quintessential human experiences.

Ptolemy suggested that each planetary sphere influences human development during a particular period of life. Rudolf Steiner, in his modern account of stages of development, also attached the planets to particular phases of life. We include some discussion of these phases to help develop an intuition for the qualities associated with each planet. However, it is important to note that these qualities are not restricted to their corresponding phase. Some people may naturally have more Saturn qualities in their character. Certain situations may bring out your Mars qualities. Bringing awareness to these qualities and developing a sense for where each one lives in us can provide an important clue for how best to engage with the world.

We have devoted a chapter in this book to each of the seven planets that captures the essential qualities of that planet, treating each as an archetypal force that acts on and through each of us. As needed, we have included additional associations to create a full picture of these forces. For instance, the classical planets have been linked to certain metals, bodily organs, days of the week, and even fairy tales, and examining their qualities can enrich the picture of the corresponding archetype. Also, we have incorporated examples from a wide range of sources, including psychological research, work with clients, and personal anecdotes to highlight how these forces can play out in daily life. Whether or not you imagine that the planets are anything more than objects in the sky, we think that reviving the language of the planets provides a fresh way of looking at social encounters that can bring renewed interest in yourself and others, and (along with it) compassion, empathy, and social engagement.

How to Approach This Book

We hope that by now it is clear that this is not your average book. It is designed to be a workbook, an opportunity for self-discovery. Each chapter provides break points with prompts that invite you to stop and reflect on your own experiences with this inner soul-ar system. We have been intentional with these prompts and their placement, so please do pause for them. Most of them ask you to find an experience from your past that has certain qualities. When you identify such an experience, try to live back into it as best you can: What was the setting, and what did it look like? Who were you with? What brought you to that place, and where did it take you? You may sometimes find it difficult to identify an experience that fits, but if you give it a little time, something usually appears. You might even start living back into an experience that doesn't quite fit the prompt; perhaps you will find that a better option suddenly appears. Many readers find it useful to keep a journal of the experiences that come to mind, what they remember about them, and what they discover as they work through them.

If possible, we recommend working with a partner or book club where you can share those stories with each other and gradually build the picture of your biography. This way of working can help provide a richer picture of the planetary qualities, particularly if some members of the group bring additional knowledge (e.g., mythology). This group process can also help you brainstorm other ways in which these qualities operate in the world or underlie important social issues. But the greatest benefit of working with others is the insight that can be gained by offering and receiving stories in a safe and inviting space—this can create tremendous feelings of empathy, gratitude, interest, and love, as if there is something deep inside you that knows that you are touching on a fundamental human experience.

In order to lay the groundwork for this experience, it is important to create a space that is safe, comfortable, and light where people feel as if they can let down their defenses to others as well as to themselves. Each group may have their own way of creating and holding that space, but it is often useful to establish some agreements at the outset about how you will share and how you will hold each other's story in confidence.

Following are four basic agreements that we often work with:

1. Know that you are in control of what you choose to share with others.

2. Practice deep, openhearted, nonjudgmental listening.

3. Respect silence as a valuable teacher.

4. Observe confidentiality, knowing that others
    shared their story as part of their work, not for
    your information.

One final note about working with this book is that you don't need to work through it in order. Each chapter is meant to stand on its own and to create the appropriate mood. So if a chapter title stands out to you, it's okay to jump ahead and start there. You also don't need to read through the whole book in one go. Feel free to put it back on the shelf and pick it up when it calls to you again. You'll find that even the same chapter has more depth and nuance than you remember once you've given it time to rest. On that note, we invite you to dive into the work to learn how the hummingbird principle works in you.

1

MOON

What Do I Need to Become Who I Am?

ONE WAY OF EXPRESSING WHO WE ARE IS THROUGH THE OBJECTS we surround ourselves with. Whether the focal point of your living room is a big-screen television, a piece of fine art, or your collection of porcelain dolls, these objects remind you of something that brings you satisfaction, and they communicate something about you to your guests. The same could be said for your taste in fashion, the landscaping in your garden, or your choice of vehicle. In this way, we can use our "outer space" as a reflection of our "inner space," and there can be a feeling of resonance when the outer and inner spaces are in harmony.

However, objects may enter our spaces that are not a reflection of our inner vision of ourselves. Friends and relatives give thoughtful gifts, and we don't have the heart to let them go even if we would never have chosen them for ourselves. Or perhaps we're lured by products that claim to make life easier and more comfortable—such as gadgets for preparing food, cleaning house, or entertainment. Other things we may fear letting go of in case we someday need them—"It's better to have it and not need it than to need it and not have it," as the saying goes. To cope with it all, you can buy organizational systems to sort everything out and store it, and you can rent self-storage units for the things that no longer fit in your house. When you start feeling overwhelmed, you can even hire an expert to come in and help you efficiently organize everything to make it feel more manageable. At some point, you might begin to wonder, "Has all this stuff really made my life easier? Has it saved me time? Has it brought me closer to being who I want to be and doing what I want to do?"

Take a moment to look around at the things in the room where you are right now. Find one thing that you love, that completely resonates with your inner self. Now find one thing that you do not like, that feels incoherent with your inner self. Is there a different feeling that arises for you when you consider those two things?

The Birth of Inner Space and Outer Space

Where does the reflection of inner space and outer space begin? Its roots can be traced back to the beginning of life. When children enter this world as infants, they are received into a space that has been prepared for them. Perhaps there is a nursery, as well as soft clothes, warm blankets, and so on. Others have selected whatever is there for them—the outer space is curated by others. Even a child's name—one of the most important and defining qualities of an individual—was given to them. It will be some time before they can select for themselves what they surround themselves with. In the meantime, their standard is comfort, and their cry is their way of providing feedback on the accommodations.

If you have ever been in the same space as an infant, you know that although their bodies are small, their spiritual presence is huge. They can permeate any space with a sense of awe, wonder, and reverence. Their tiny cries can bring all activity to a halt, and their little gummy smiles can make any heart melt. For adults who have (or anticipate) such experiences, there can be a strong tendency to bring a materialistic offering of gratitude. Babies are "showered" with gifts—clothing, stuffed animals, blankets, colorful mobiles, electronics with flashing lights that blip and bloop. And of course there are whole industries built up around telling parents what they need to buy so their children can be safe and happy and intelligent and strong. With minimal awareness on their parents' part, children's spaces can become cluttered and over-stimulating, impacting what the children experience as normal, and blurring the line between need and superfluousness.

Through such expressions, children can also begin to see relationships in transactional terms, and thus look forward to visits from relatives not for love and companionship, but for the gifts they expect to receive. Parents might cringe when they hear their child ask someone, "What are you bringing me?" but it is the child's honest reaction to how they have learned the world works. As children grow and mature, they can then tether their self-worth to their property and the gifts they continue to receive from others.

On the other side of this spectrum, some children are born into circumstances where their needs are barely or inconsistently met. In most of these cases, children's material needs are covered, but the children might internalize a lack of interest, loving warmth, or a heart-based connection. It is important to note that this end of the spectrum is not necessarily related to material poverty, but rather to the social atmosphere that envelops the child. For example, a child who is tended to by a string of nannies who do not take an interest in them can experience this kind of "soul poverty." The same can be true for caregivers dealing with serious personal issues, such as addiction, depression, trauma, unemployment, or relationship difficulties.

To summarize the gesture of this age, the outer space filled by the child is gradually drawn inward, and the quality of that space shapes the inner qualities of the child. This process continues through the early childhood years, which last until approximately age seven. For children whose outer spaces are defined by materialistic goods, the inner space can become filled with materialistic concerns and ideas, which may not leave enough space to develop oneself as a unique individual. Consequently, they can be slower to "grow up," and they can remain dependent on others for a much longer time. For children whose spaces are defined by emptiness, that emptiness does not nurture their natural development but instead demands that they grow up more rapidly to take responsibility for themselves to survive. In both cases, there can be a quality of coldness involved. However, the quality of the middle path is warmth, due to the presence of heart-based connection, genuine interest, and the overarching question, "What do you need to become who you are?"

> What was the warmth quality of your early childhood experience? If you could put a temperature on it, what would it be? If you have siblings, do you think they would report a similar temperature? You might want to ask them.

The Bright Side and the Dark Side

When this connection between possessions and self-worth is established, individuals may try to compensate for inner insecurities or private struggles by surrounding themselves with material goods that signal to themselves and others that everything is just fine—a process that psychologists refer to as "symbolic self-completion."[13] This projection of a "bright side"—a persona that attempts to mask or override a "dark side" that holds pain, suffering, uncertainty, inadequacy, or isolation—can contribute to both personal and social complications. The psychologist Carl Jung warned that people can come to identify with this persona, preferring it to the true self or believing it to be the true self.[14] He stated:

> [H]enceforth he lives exclusively against the background of his own biography. . . . One could say, with a little exaggeration, that the persona is that which in reality one is not, but which oneself as well as others think one is.[15]

Knowing your own personal struggle while perceiving that everyone else is doing just fine can exacerbate your stress and make you feel even more alone. On the social side, as individuals project this bright side and identify with it, they can become more protective of the secrets of their dark sides. As a consequence, they may resist the kinds of interdependence—both formal (as in close relationships) and informal (as in neighborhoods)—that could both provide social support and show them that they are not alone in struggling to cope with the modern world.

Drawing on Jungian ideas, the psychoanalyst Robert Johnson says that everyone has a shadow side that arises through the process of socialization.[16] Essentially, children learn that there are certain ways of being that promote social harmony and civilization within that culture, and in doing so they learn that certain tendencies need to be suppressed or concealed. These suppressed and concealed tendencies become the shadow, which continues to work within us in unconscious ways. Importantly, Johnson states that even positive characteristics can work their way into the shadow if they don't meet the conditions of social acceptability:

> Some of the pure gold of our personality is relegated to the shadow because it can find no place in that great leveling process that is culture. . . . The gold is related to our higher calling, and this can be hard to accept at certain stages of life. Ignoring the gold can be as damaging as ignoring the dark side of the psyche, and some people may suffer a severe shock or illness before they learn how to let the gold out.[17]

Johnson argues that the shadow is both unavoidable and potentially productive, and that the challenge is to learn how to bring it into the light for oneself and transform its restraining energy into productive energy.

Becoming Selfie-ish

There is another way that the bright side/dark side distinction plays out in our modern world: the phenomenon of the "selfie." Modern technology allows photographs to be taken and shared with the online world any time and any place, which has given rise to the selfie as a form of self-expression. It is not uncommon to see individuals stopping to take a selfie while walking their dog, riding the bus, or sitting at a café table. And while the settings may make it seem like the photos were casual and impromptu, the ability to screen photos immediately and discard all but the best enables individuals to "put their best face forward," so to speak. As a form of expression, selfies are a way to let one's bright side shine and to celebrate travel, time spent with friends, and other positive experiences. Just as it can be healthy to have a physical space that is well curated to reflect your inner self, it can be good to have a digital presence that expresses who you are to your friends and followers.

However, there can be dark sides to selfies as well, and they are related to some of the issues we have already discussed. For many, sharing selfies on social media is linked to an expectation for positive reactions from friends, usually in the form of "likes" and positive comments. In such cases, the photo becomes more than an expression—it becomes a plea for validation. If a post fails to elicit the desired response, the individual can be deeply hurt. This hurt represents another consequence of identifying with the persona, and it can be particularly painful when the cheerful and polished façade is concealing inner pain or insecurity. Perhaps it is even the case that identifying strongly with the persona and relying on external cues for validation are responsible for a "hollowing out" of the inner space, and an outward turning of the inner mirror to know who you really are.

The proliferation of selfies on social media may also perpetuate a sense that everyone is doing awesome—except me. Social media provides an ideal platform for projecting a highly refined image of oneself, and even if you know that others are being selective in how they represent themselves in those spaces, your uncertainty about how much distortion is present can interfere with your ability to adjust accordingly. What is needed here is the inner strength to not judge yourself against the standards set by others. Instead, you must look inwardly to find not only your own personal standard but also the willingness to share your dark side with some close and trusted confidants. For a life buoy in such circumstances, we can remember the adage, "Don't compare your insides to someone else's outsides."

Qualities of the Moon

Few heavenly bodies have been the subject of as much study and contemplation as the Moon. This mysterious body, which moves across the sky each night, changes its apparent form as it progresses through the lunar cycle, and draws the waters of the seas up and down twice daily. Life on Earth would certainly not be the same without it.

If we rely on our own faculties of perception, what can we say about the Moon? We could note, first and foremost, that it is most visible during the night, when the brightness of the Sun has retreated from our part of the Earth. In this vein, the Moon has been associated with the qualities of the night, such as silence and stillness. The experience of the stillness of the night can make the space around us feel more spacious, which can inspire feelings from awe to tranquility to dread.

We could also observe that the pattern of luminosity varies in a cyclical way from new to full and back again. In fact, the Moon is strongly connected with rhythm, including the rhythm of the tides and the close relationship between the lunar cycle and women's menstrual cycle. As one example of how people have attended to the Moon's rhythms, farmers have long organized their planting and harvesting schedules according to the lunar rhythm. The thirteen Moon cycles of the lunar year were given names such as Harvest Moon or Hay Moon to indicate the focal tasks of the month and even the appropriateness of a given activity. This attention to cosmic rhythms is perhaps most visible now as part of the biodynamic agriculture movement, but it belongs to the conventional wisdom of farmers, and lunar phases are still commonly included in farmers' almanacs.

The cause of the phases is the particular relationship in space between the Earth, Moon, and Sun, which changes gradually over the 29.5-day cycle. It is, of course, the Sun's light that we see reflecting off of the Moon, and mirroring and reflection are common qualities ascribed to the Moon. Correspondingly, the metal silver has been associated with the Moon. Like the Moon, a silver mirror produces a reflected image that we could say is "cooler" than the original object, meaning it lacks warmth. Silver was essential in the development of photography, and photographs (like memories) are often experienced as a poor (although sometimes necessary) substitute for the "real thing." This feeling of coldness may come from the fact that the object is not directly present in what we see, but has been removed from the present, with its primary existence in the past. In viewing the image, we work to rekindle the warmth of the object.

Another peculiar feature of the Moon that is easily observed is that the same face is always visible to us here on Earth. This feature gives rise to what are commonly referred to as the bright side and the dark side of the Moon; the bright side is the one that we can see, and the dark side is the one that is oriented away from Earth. This fact translates into qualities like mystery or secrecy, as well as polarities such as light vs. shadow, outer vs. inner, public vs. private. Of course, the dark side of the Moon is not actually dark. Instead, when we experience a new moon on Earth, the dark side is completely bathed in sunlight. The apparent darkness is due to our limited vantage point, and we might ask how to step out of that perspective to see other parts illuminated.

The phase of life that Rudolf Steiner associated with the Moon is early childhood (birth to age 7). In this phase, we can see clear parallels with the Moon qualities outlined above. Young children thrive on rhythm and predictability, and parents and teachers who create strong daily, weekly, and seasonal rhythms will see that the children find comfort and security in that predictability. During this time, learning happens primarily through imitation, which relates to the qualities of mirroring and reflection. Just like the Moon, young children take in all that radiates toward them from the outside world, and they will reflect back whatever they receive (including some phrases and behaviors parents wish they wouldn't!). Development during the Moon years is the most generic. Babies from all cultures start from a similar point and work toward the same general milestones in the first years of life—walking, talking, and thinking—and the individuality of the child (both in physical appearance and in soul qualities) only gradually begins to emerge during this time.

Working with Moon Forces in Daily Life:
Moon Minutes

When we were born, space wasn't just—*BOOM*—there! We had to start by being very close to our mothers and moving in "baby steps" from there outward into the space of life: Mum–crib–room–house–garden–street–neighborhood–village–city–school.

The same happens when we begin to wake up to our own space and find out that it is either overloaded with stuff or still not set up, even though we have lived in the same place for several years. You can sense the disharmony between your outer and inner space and instantly feel overwhelmed by the scope of the problem. You sink back into your armchair, and years can pass while the problem gets bigger. If you find yourself in this situation, you can start to work with the concept of Moon Minutes, which are built from two of the key qualities of Moon: rhythm and quiet patience.

You can begin by taking a look around and becoming aware of what there is. No judgment, no starting yet, but a patient, objective gaze around into the space: What do I feel? Is my space coherent with who I am? After completing this scan, you can decide to focus on one little thing: the dishes in the sink, a dirty window, a painting still not hung, a pile of papers to sort through, dirty clothes, gifts you never wanted but don't know what to do with, dried out flowers. Pick just one thing, estimate the number of Moon Minutes you need, and do it. Then sit back down and feel your inner space. Did something shift?

The basic idea of Moon Minutes is to use the power of rhythm in a comforting and manageable way. You could decide, for instance, that every Monday you will dedicate just ten Moon Minutes to improving your space. Part of the secret of Moon Minutes is that rhythm can compensate for lack of strength, so if you find you cannot muster the willpower to tackle the task all at once, you might find that by consciously incorporating these Moon Minutes into your daily or weekly rhythm, they gradually become a part of your habit life—you may even begin to look forward to them in the time in between. This time in between is also part of the Moon Minutes, as the patience is as necessary as the doing. Why? When we go back to the first seven years of life, we see that we can't speed up things. Every child reaches milestones like taking their first step and speaking their first words on their own time—there is little that parents can do to try to speed up that process. The in-between time of quiet patience is the fuel for later Moon Minutes. So whenever you become aware that your outer space needs to be realigned with your inner space, Moon Minutes can be a useful tool for how to get there.

Carve out some Moon Minutes to take out your cell phone and delete any unnecessary photos. How does it feel to declutter your digital space?

Another Way to Work with Moon Forces:
The Power of Puzzle and Wonder

I look at this life as a puzzle without all the pieces in the box.

— Jonathan Anthony Burkett

We all have certain pieces of the puzzle missing in our lives. Even if parents did their best, it is impossible to give children everything they need. Why is that? Well, first, as every parent is aware, there is no instruction manual for raising children—although the bookstores have endless shelves of guides for parents to think otherwise. In addition, all people are individuals who will develop out of and into themselves in the course of life, and that means that parents do not control all of the pieces in the first place.

These missing puzzle pieces can include anything that was not covered in early childhood—for example, if you did not learn how to style your long hair, or if you grew up in an area with minimal cultural diversity—making it feel more difficult later in life. It can also be that your parents were frequently absent, so you did not receive adequate attention or recognition. Everything that is missing can have an origin in the early years of life, and this lack can spur us on to become active and creative later in life in service of becoming ourselves. The psychologist Alfred Adler (who is credited with coining the term "lifestyle") suggested that in early childhood we begin to develop a prototypic way of handling our "inferiorities" (i.e., missing pieces), one of which involves working to transform those limitations into strengths.[18] As with any puzzle, all the pieces have value, and the hardest thing to do is to find the missing pieces in a box. Much time and energy can be spent maintaining the semblance of perfection. As little sense as it makes to ignore the missing pieces, it makes just as little sense to throw away pieces that can't yet be fit into the rest of the picture.

How can we use the qualities of the Moon to grow with this imperfection? We need a special power that is highly active especially in early childhood. It is the ability to wonder! In wonder, you have to hold yourself back a bit and thereby create a little space for something new to enter. For example, instead of casting judgment on someone's unconventional fashion sense, you can invite wonder and maybe decide to try something new yourself. Or if you realize that networking at a business conference is uncomfortable for you, instead of immediately indulging your own malaise and shutting down, if you can step back and marvel about it first, you can create space for a possible encounter. This ability to invoke wonder can be invaluable throughout the puzzle-building process of life: I wonder what that experience was meant to teach me. I wonder why she spoke so rudely to me. I wonder what I'll be doing when I meet my life partner.

A little story can illustrate this. Several years ago, Anne traveled with her sister from Switzerland to the US, and right from the beginning things did not go according to plan. They missed all of their connecting flights and instead of thirteen hours of traveling, they finally arrived after twenty-three hours! Her sister couldn't understand Anne's peace and serenity and lamented loudly. Anne explained that instead of feeling frustrated, she was turning to her sense of wonder: I wonder why all of this is happening right now and what good might come out of it? Two months later, they were both refunded half of their airfare by the airline, right when they both needed the money urgently. Such developments are possible when one practices wonder.

> Think about a situation where something didn't work out the way it was planned but later turned into something even better. Or maybe you missed an opportunity to do something you had been hoping to do, only to find that you would have had a bad experience if you had gone. Did you find the power of wonder in that situation? How might it have been different if you had?

The ability to wonder that we received in our early childhood can help us look forward into the future with a refreshing, cooling, renewing, and life-giving perspective. It allows us to see the storms of life as potentially having a silver lining. The sense of wonder can feel like morning dew, a refreshment from the night, greetings from the Moon! The more we wonder, the more we build up the capacity in ourselves to work creatively with the puzzle pieces we have been given and patiently await the moment when we find missing pieces or find new ways of fitting in ones that have kept us guessing. One can attract new situations and new opportunities through sheer wonder. Try it!

Beyond Expectations

Kids these days are stressed out. It's true of college students (such as the ones Chris works with) who worry about grades and athletics and landing a good job, but stress and anxiety seem to reach further back into childhood every year. If you've ever seen a kindergartener wheeling a backpack full of books to school, you can begin to understand why. At the core is a certain ideology that sees children as essentially incomplete or undereducated adults, and that the sooner we can begin the process of filling them up with knowledge and skills, the more productive citizens they'll grow up to be. So, from an increasingly early age, adults expect children to learn to read and perform arithmetic and play sports and music and even absorb the foundational logic for computer coding. In some cases, these expectations are codified as part of standardized tests. And, in what might seem absurd to an observer from an older generation, some kindergartens have entrance exams that require children, among other things, to be able write their name and read basic sight words.

In a 2016 article,[19] education researcher Daphna Bassok and her colleagues provide evidence of the dramatic shifts in kindergarten since the turn of the twenty-first century. Using data from a large-scale longitudinal study, they show marked increases in kindergarten teachers' academic expectations for kindergarteners and the amount of time they spent on academic content, as well as decreases in time spent on artistic activities and unstructured, child-driven activities. They link these shifts to changes in education policy, such as the No Child Left Behind (NCLB) Act of 2001, which was meant to decrease the achievement gap by increasing the accountability of schools. With the stakes of student performance on standardized tests raised, schools devoted an increasing amount of time to preparing students for the exams, often at the expense of arts and physical education. And while NCLB has become a sort of lightning rod among advocates for educational reform, in many ways it only amplified the trends of higher academic expectations for children from an increasingly young age. Like the kindergarten teachers from the survey, there is a growing feeling that children should be able to learn more from an earlier age, and that it is good for them if they do.

The psychologist Peter Gray highlighted the implications of these trends for children's mental health in a 2011 article in the *American Journal of Play*.[20] He traces the decline of free play among children much farther back—to the transition from the hunter-gatherer to agrarian lifestyles, when children's responsibilities to their families became more solidified. In terms of more recent history (when more data are readily available), he points to the first half of the twentieth century as a time when children's time for free play was at a peak. Since the middle of the twentieth century, parents have exerted increasing control over children's time, with a particularly striking decline in children's unstructured time with friends outside of organized activities like sports teams. Older readers of this book may recall rules from their childhoods like, "Be home before the streetlights come on," while today groups of unsupervised children in public are virtually nonexistent. Paralleling this decline in free play, says Gray, is a large increase in mental health problems among children and adolescents, from higher anxiety and depression to a decreased sense of personal control and even higher rates of suicide. And while Gray notes that establishing a firm causal link between these two trends is very difficult, he makes a compelling case for the mental health protective effects of unstructured free play.

And in perhaps the clearest demonstration yet that these increased academic expectations of young children are misplaced, a recent study by Vanderbilt University researcher Kelley Durkin and her colleagues[21] shows that any gains from this early intervention are eliminated or even reversed by the end of elementary school. The researchers looked at the outcomes of a state-funded prekindergarten program in Tennessee. Because there were not enough spaces in the program for all who were eligible, children were randomly selected to participate. This selection process created a strong comparison between the children receiving the intervention and an equivalent control group who did not participate. They found that by third grade, those who participated in the program had lower standardized test scores on reading, math, and science than those in the control group, with the differences growing over time. They also found that sixth-grade students from the program were more likely to have an IEP (individualized educational program, a marker of special education status) than those who did not participate. Finally, those who participated in the program had higher rates of disciplinary infractions by third grade, and the discrepancy grew over time. Durkin and colleagues suggest that one explanation for the washing out of the initial benefits of such programs is their focus on "constrained skills" like teaching the letters of the alphabet versus "unconstrained skills" such as attention and self-control, which allow for continued growth when confronting new challenges.

From the vantage point of Moon, these early academic expectations are out of alignment with natural processes of growth and maturation. If we imagine that the child is a tree that we want to grow up big and strong and capable and resilient, we must first take time to nourish the roots, and second, we must allow it time to grow at a natural pace. If instead, we clip the roots as if it were a bonsai and give it artificial fertilizer to quicken the rate of growth, we might find the appearance of early rapid growth, but the first strong gust of wind might be enough to throw off branches or topple the whole tree.

What is it that tempts us to cut childhood short? Society's expectations of the individual are complex and weigh heavily. Every child has to play an instrument, do well in school, play sports, have friends, study, earn enough money later, look good, be friendly, know good from bad, speak a foreign language, make their parents proud, be well-adjusted yet individual, learn with joy and, last but not least, do better than their parents. You get tired just listing them. But in various spoken and unspoken ways, we get the message that it's the right thing to do to give the child the best start. Especially in an environment where higher education is seen as necessary for any chance of a successful future, parents can feel compelled to adopt these expectations to give their child a competitive advantage for the long run. But when these expectations creep into the time when children are still experiencing themselves as part of the unity of the world, they can experience these interventions as a "rude awakening."

What is an expectation? An expectation is a belief that something should happen in a particular way, or that someone or something should have particular qualities or behaviors. Expectation, then, is a limited view of events or developments that are supposed to occur in the future. But what is it like with a child? Can we expect anything at all? Is it worthwhile to invest in the child in order to fulfill these expectations, even if they are of sublime quality? How do we know what a child is capable of and where their potential or interest lies? Let's take a short trip back in time to a man who literally accepted his own death in order to shield the orphan children in his care from the painful reality of the adult world.

Janusz Korczak (1878–1942) was a Polish military doctor and pediatrician. He was also a successful writer and had a great social commitment to poor and neglected children. In 1912, he was offered a position building and managing a Jewish orphanage in Warsaw. He gave up his medical profession and accepted the position, which was to become his life's work. He introduced a pedagogical structure based on what he viewed as the fundamental rights of children, and thus he broke new ground. When the First World War began, he was called up as a divisional doctor in the Russian army, during which time wrote his main work: *How to Love a Child*.[22] He returned after the war and took charge of a second orphanage.

When the Second World War broke out, the orphanage had to move to the Warsaw Ghetto. On August 5, 1942, the orphanage's approximately two hundred children were deported by the SS (the Nazi party's combat branch) and sent to the Treblinka extermination camp. Although Janusz Korczak knew that it meant his death, he did not want to abandon his children, so he insisted on going with them. The composer and pianist Władysław Szpilman was an eyewitness to the deportation and describes the scene in his memoirs:

One day, around August 5 . . . I happened to witness the departure of Janusz Korczak and his orphans from the ghetto. For that morning the "evacuation" of the Jewish orphanage, of which Janusz Korczak was the director, had been ordered; he himself had the opportunity to save himself, and only with difficulty did he get the Germans to allow him to accompany the children. He had spent long years of his life with children and even now, on his last journey, he did not want to leave them alone. He wanted to make it easier for them. They would go to the country, a reason for joy, he explained to the orphans. At last they could exchange the hideous, stuffy walls for meadows where flowers grew, for streams where they could bathe, for forests where there were so many berries and mushrooms.

He ordered them to dress festively and so, nicely dressed up, in a cheerful mood, they entered the courtyard in pairs. The small column was led by an SS man who, as a German, loved children, even those whom he would shortly send to the afterlife. He particularly liked a twelve-year-old boy, a violinist, who carried his instrument under his arm. He ordered him to step forward at the head of the children's procession and play—and so they set off. When I met them at Gęsia Street, the children, beaming, were singing in chorus, the little musician was playing for them, and Korczak was carrying two of the smallest ones, who were also smiling, in his arms and telling them something funny. Certainly, still in the gas chamber, when the cyclone was already choking the childish throats and fear was taking the place of joy and hope in the hearts of the orphans, the "Old Doctor" whispered with the last effort: "Nothing, it's nothing, children," in order to spare at least his little pupils the horror of the transition from life to death.[23]

Janusz Korczak knew about the soul of the child. In *How to Love a Child*, he called for a *magna carta libertatis* of three basic rights for children, which, in our terms, can enable the transition from Expectation to Beyond Expectation. First, the child has the right to die. This may seem unusual at first, but how much experience of themselves and the world are children denied on account of "keeping them safe"? Korczak says, "Fearful that the child may be snatched from us by death, we snatch from him life; not wanting him to die, we won't let him live." What this means is that risk and daring are also part of a child's life. One cannot and must not let children grow up in a totally protected world. In a white room with white furniture and white-clothed figures, only an anemic, pale child can grow. Of course, we do not mean to imply that adults should neglect their children or subject them to harm or undue risk. Rather, it is an invitation to allow the child to learn through participating with the world to develop in their fullness.

Second, every child has the right to the present day. Says Korczak: "The educator is not obliged to take upon himself the responsibility for a distant future, but he is fully responsible for today." The day is a stage in the here and now, and whoever constantly aims only at the future will miss their mark. It is important not to lose sight of this, even in today's world, because whoever takes the time to let the children be as they are, giving them time to try and figure things out for themselves, will realize that we can learn a lot from them. To see the child as they are right now and to let them be that person frees the child from the grip of right and wrong ways of being or doing.

And third, every child has the right to be the way they are. You can't make a boisterous, loud child into a quiet, reserved child, and you can't do it the other way around either. Nor is it necessary to drag the child's potential out into the light of day if they simply don't want to. Such "stubbornness" often leads to frustration on the part of the parents, but isn't it actually a failure to perceive the child as they are? Korczak quips, "Cheer up, caregiver. You're already casting off your prejudiced, sentimental view of the child. You already know that you don't know. It's not like you believed, so things are different. Not getting by, you're already looking for a way. Are you getting lost? . . . Are you suffering? The truth is born in pain."[24]

What these three postulates point out is that looking after the fundamental dignity of the child is much more about adopting a sense of openness and wonder toward the child than trying to protect them against the cruel world. All expectations are thrown overboard when these three rights are addressed. But what do we gain when we leave expectations behind? That is, what awaits us in the space beyond expectation? Beyond expectation is the freedom for the child to become the person they were meant to develop into, a heightened sensitivity to the unique gifts, talents, and struggles that each child carries into this life, and an awakening of new possibilities within ourselves when we step out of the role of protector of the future grownup. By Korczak's measure, the best way to serve the future-grownups is to let go of that idea altogether and simply allow them to be today's child. After all, the future that the child will face is yet unknown to us. There will be problems we are not yet aware of and solutions we cannot yet imagine. What can happen when we embrace the possibility that the gifts that our child came to give back to the world are ones we are not yet able to fathom?

2

MERCURY

The "Just-Because" Impulse

WHO DOESN'T DREAM OF THEIR PERFECT WEDDING, THE MOST beautiful children's birthday party, the most romantic marriage proposal, or the perfect vacation? But wishes alone are not enough to bring these dreams into reality.

For instance, consider the wedding. There are many unwritten rules in planning a wedding, and care has to be taken so that everything runs smoothly, that all of the guests' needs are met, and that everyone has as much fun as you can imagine. If it's your first wedding, you don't know what you don't know, but maybe you know that there's a lot you don't. The day is coming, and everything has to be perfect—it is, after all, the most important day of your life. Expectations are high and a lot of time and money have been invested in this moment. A small mistake can turn into a catastrophe. So you do what seems reasonable: you start hiring professionals to plan everything. From the decorations to the menu to the music playlist, they take care of it all. Ah! You breathe a sigh of relief. Everything is planned, scripted, and made to look effortless. Everything, that is, except for the unpredictable mistakes and failures. A fragile framework of daydreams is carried into reality, and the pressure of perfection can eclipse the joy in the planning process as well as the event itself.

Years later, when you remember this day, what traces will be left from all the scripted and outsourced elements of the event? Most likely they will have faded into the background because everything that could have become permanent in them was exhausted in the preparation. Through this preparation—the plotting of how great everything would be—it became impossible to lead the event through the present, and the past (planning) was linked directly to the future (memory). And in order to keep things just so, the event became a choreographed performance that might have evoked a feeling of boredom from performers and audience alike. Of course, boredom can lead to creativity, but pseudo-creativity that leads to boredom can drain the life out of an experience. What you will remember most clearly from the day are the unexpected things. The tears in your father's eyes as he walked you down the aisle. The brief rain shower that had everyone scrambling for cover, then laughing about it. The uncle who had a few too many drinks before cutting up the dance floor. These unplanned moments restore the human element to the event and are what really make it your special day. You wouldn't trade surprises like these for all the planning in the world.

Or consider a bachelorette party, where a group of women engage in a night of boisterous debauchery. Before setting out, everyone puts on a crown and sash so people outside the group can clearly see that this behavior is part of a planned celebration or "scripted fun," so to speak. Being so recognizable promotes tolerance among bystanders: "Oh, let them have their fun, it's just a bachelorette party." With the crown on, anything can happen, including activities that nobody in the group really enjoys to begin with. Sure, it's what you're supposed to do, but is it really the kind of fun you're looking for? Once you've hung up your crown for the night, will you look back on the experience fondly or with a tinge of embarrassment, hoping that nobody outside of the group recognized you?

In the over-planned wedding or the prescribed bachelorette party, the power of spontaneity, the ability to take mistakes in stride, and the ability to be open to whatever this moment wants to become are sacrificed in service of predictability and peace of mind. Learning to relinquish some measure of control and invite the unexpected can relieve the burden of getting it just right and create more opportunities for genuine, *unscripted* fun.

This is where the secret of Mercury lies hidden.

> Take a moment to find three experiences in your life that are fun to remember. What about those experiences made them so fun? Were they fully scripted, semi-scripted, or not scripted at all?

Tag, You're It!

The thought of fun might immediately take us back to childhood, with memories of adventures with friends or siblings bubbling to the surface.

Childish fun reaches its peak in the middle phase of childhood—from about 7 to 14 years old—as the dreamy consciousness of the young child is suffused with imagination and social creativity. These children are enchanted by fantasy worlds and can often be found with their noses buried in books that take them to unknown places. In these worlds, anything is possible, and the child's powers of imagination are fostered by the fantastic creatures, dynamic actions, and elaborate storylines. These books (or comic books or video games) are fodder for the elaborate games and role-plays that they create on the playground. If you ever watch children playing (or perhaps you have memories from your own childhood), you'll notice that the children rarely articulate the rules of their games explicitly, except maybe to assign roles, and even those can morph and change on the fly in the course of the play. In fact, it's the preformed games with rules that are often sources of conflict, as one child's sensitivity to unfairness bumps into another's need for fluidity. In the next minute, the children are playing beautifully again, and five minutes later the roles reverse. It can be a time of volatility in the life of feelings, but the big feelings tend to depart as quickly as they arrived. The natural state of being during this phase is fluidity, cocreativity, and movement.

Of course, this period also corresponds with school age, with the better part of it overlapping with the primary or elementary school years. And though the child is capable of academic learning at this time, the general structure of many school environments runs counter to this natural state of being. Movement is replaced by sitting still for hours on end. Fluidity is replaced by "These are the facts" and "This is the way it is." The impulse to cocreate with others is replaced by a focus on individual aptitude and evaluation. It may be no wonder that so many children these days are stressed out and have trouble sitting still and staying focused at school. In a popular TED Talk, Sir Kenneth Robinson argues that the structure and one-sidedness of educational systems stifles the inherent creativity of children.[25] And it does so to our own detriment, as these children will grow into adults who will need to solve problems we cannot yet imagine.

In contrast to early childhood, where learning happens primarily through imitation and repetition, learning in middle childhood is grounded in experience, rhythm, and movement. For instance, learning multiplication tables may prove elusive until the child learns an appropriate clapping game or jump rope rhyme. By connecting the "facts" to their bodies in a rhythmic way, the facts don't just live in their heads—children can feel them in their whole bodies. One of the most important aspects of learning during this phase is the possibility of failure. That is, children learn how things work by learning how they don't work. They learn something about physics when their bridge made of sticks collapses. They learn something about music theory when they hit a note that doesn't fit with the others. And they learn something about botany when they forget to water their seedlings and the plants wilt. Failure that is allowed to unfold free of self-consciousness or criticism can be a powerful teacher and a wellspring of creativity. When the task is structured so that the possibility of failure is removed, the child may have a superficial experience of "success," but the lesson also remains on the surface, and the child is not likely to return to the same task a second time. Achieving success through trial-and-error leads to deeper learning and a much stronger experience of satisfaction—and it's more fun!

We see in this phase, as in adulthood, that Mercury has a tendency to get squeezed out. On the one hand, children may be coddled and protected, prevented from learning through exploration and experience in this way. They have "helicopter parents" who do everything in their power to protect their child from disappointment, injury, and failure. On the other hand, children may be pushed forward into an adolescent consciousness, where they are fed abstract knowledge and big truths about the world that they don't yet know what to do with. We can see that early childhood is connected more to the past and adolescence is more connected to the future. Middle childhood, along with all themes related to Mercury, is about the present (and presence), and we can get a feeling for how precarious the present really is, as well as how freedom is only possible in the present. The author Hugh Prather said, "Tomorrow is shallow, but today is as deep as truth."[26] The right now is where all of the possibilities reside. Importantly, though, the right now is never static. You can't sit comfortably in the present—before your bottom hits the seat, the chair has already been moved. Holding onto the present is an active state that requires constant movement, and it's hard to hold on in a world that so easily drops anchor in the past or the future.

That said, children in this age range are also yearning for some "definites" about life. Whereas in early childhood they experienced themselves as a unity with the world, they awaken here to the reality of their separateness from the world—there is "me" and there is "not me." This feeling of separateness means many things for the child, but two of the primary consequences are a need to know the "ground rules" of life, and a recognition that positive relationships with others are not simply given. The latter we see evidence of at home and school, that children want parents and teachers to be pleased with them, and that they may learn that their value is tied to their behavior or the quality of their work. While these kinds of reinforcements can motivate positive engagements, they may also contribute to what psychologist Carl Rogers referred to as *conditions of worth*—a feeling that one's value in the eyes of others depends on one's actions or achievements.[27] Rogers links creativity (for which he saw a desperate need) to unconditional positive regard—the feeling of being loved and valued regardless of abilities or accomplishments.[28]

The other consequence of the feeling of separateness is the need for clear boundary conditions, and we see this often in children's emphasis on rules and enforcing fairness. For as much as children in the middle years enjoy freedom and fluidity, they need a clear structure to work within—freedom within form. When they experience shifting standards, double standards, or inconsistently applied expectations (e.g., with younger siblings), they are quick to cry foul and slow to relent. As with the children's naive conception of time, adults cannot reason with them that their sense of fairness is incomplete. Neither can adults always understand children's conception of fairness. The children may be happily engaged in a game that appears patently unfair to an observing grownup—for instance, a game of "monkey in the middle" where the smallest child is in the middle. If the adult tries to intervene and make the game fairer, it could ruin the game for everyone (including the ones on the receiving end of the unfairness). In both cases, the children are not looking to the adults to make the situation fairer, but rather are allowing themselves to enter into the experience of unfairness and to learn from it.

What kinds of stories were you drawn to in your middle childhood years? These might have been books, television programs, your grandfather's stories, or comics. What was it that attracted you to these stories, and where do they live in you now?

False Pretenses

Pretending is a quintessential Mercury quality. In childhood, it is perfectly natural for children to freely pretend to be all kinds of things that they are not, from monsters to doctors to babies to elephants. But what role does pretending play in adult life, and is it always healthy? One way we sometimes pretend as adults is by changing our appearance or behavior to conform to what we think others are expecting of us. We invent a person who is not authentically ourselves to give people what we think they want from us. Maybe you've done it on a first date, where you pretended to share an interest in spelunking with the other person, even though you have never set foot in a cave. Then, after having a lot of fun, if they invite you to go cave diving for your second date, you're stuck. You either have to continue the deception or admit to it and risk losing the relationship. This form of pretending is reactive, where it arises out of an ongoing situation. However, sometimes we pre-pretend—we take on a role before we even enter a situation based on what we think will "go over well." And when you miscalculate and the pretend-you rubs others the wrong way, the whole thing collapses. There is nowhere to go. Once again, it is hard to regain the respect of the others by admitting you were pretending to be someone you were not. Like the boy who cried wolf, they can never be sure when you are being you and when you're trying to deceive. Here we see a shadow side of Mercury—the idea that it is necessary to take on a different character to meet the real or imagined expectations of others in a situation.

Why do we pretend in this way? We could say that there is a certain insecurity that underlies it—a feeling that the natural "you" won't be met with approval or success in the situation, or that you will even be rejected in your natural form. The pretending is a form of compensation for what we imagine (or have been told) are our shortcomings—just as the child who is not getting positive attention from peers or teachers for their academic performance can take on the role of class clown or bully to get attention in a different way. The need for approval to avoid feeling isolated and disconnected can be very strong, and this need can become crystallized into a set of expectations that leave us in a state of pretending that is decidedly not free. In fact, if we attend to the various ways that we contort ourselves to "fit in" to different situations, we may find a pattern (or even a single moment) from earlier in our lives where we learned that adaptation.

There is a fable from Aesop called "The man, the boy, and the donkey" that describes these three characters walking into town. A passerby makes a critical remark because the man and the boy were walking while a perfectly good donkey went unburdened. So the man put the boy on the donkey, and they continued on. Then someone else called the boy lazy for riding while his father walked. So they switched places, and it wasn't long before someone criticized the man as lazy for making his son walk. Then the man pulled the boy up too, and someone else chastised them for overburdening the poor donkey. So they got down, tied the donkey's feet together, attached a pole, and carried him into town on their shoulders. But as they were crossing a bridge, the donkey kicked a leg loose, causing the boy to drop his end of the pole, and the donkey fell into the river and drowned, to which an onlooker retorted, "That will teach you."

The moral of "please all and you will please none" is a good lesson for those trying to conform to what they expect others want them to be. Or perhaps you remember some of your strategies for deflecting criticism from your childhood: "I know you are but what am I?" or

"I'm rubber and you're glue, whatever you say bounces off me and sticks to you," or (plugging your ears) "Lalalalala . . . I can't hear you!" These are all ways of saying, "I know who I am, and I know that who I am is good enough."

But is there a positive role for pretending in adulthood? Sure there is. Pretending in a playful way—such as with the steampunk subculture—can be a healthy way of engaging the imagination and retaining some youthful qualities throughout adulthood. Or take an artist like David Bowie, who often took on a completely new persona when creating a new album, carrying it through not only the recordings, but also his performances and public appearances. He once said, "If you feel safe in the area you are working in, you are not working in the right area. Always go a little further into the water than you feel you are capable of being in—go a little bit out of your depth. And when you don't feel that your feet are quite touching the bottom, you are just about in the right place to do something exciting."[29]

In addition, we could say that a certain kind of inner pretending can be adaptive. For instance, maybe you need to have a medical procedure, and you're feeling scared. You know that your fear is not serving you or your health, so you decide to pretend you're brave. Maybe you concoct a story in your mind about how you were injured saving a busload of children from going over a cliff, and how you now need to bring that bravery into your medical procedure. Or maybe you are going into a job interview and feeling insecure about your ability to find the right words to answer questions effectively. So you decide to pretend that you are the interviewer, and you're the one trying to figure out if they are good enough for you. It's a strategy that is sometimes referred to as "fake it 'til you make it," and it has a distinctively Mercury quality.

All Roads Lead to Rome

One of the qualities that enables social life to work is predictability. In order to feel free in yourself, you need to feel relatively confident about what those around you are going to do. If the behavior of others was completely erratic and unpredictable, every situation would demand your full attention, you wouldn't be able to import any expectations from past situations, and you would not really be able to create or act on longer-term plans. And so, one of the basic hallmarks of civilization is the rule of law. The rule of law sets down expectations for behavior and consequences for deviation from those behaviors—from mundane behaviors such as which side of the road to drive on, to more egregious acts like murder. To be a part of a society (or even just to pay it a visit) means to implicitly agree to abide by its laws—its notions of what is fair and what is allowable. But, of course, these formal expectations are not limited to states and countries. We find rules, procedures, structures, and formalities everywhere we look: employers have handbooks to guide employee behavior; schools have codes of conduct for students; fancy restaurants have dress codes and expectations for proper etiquette. If you've ever visited a major city like New York, you will find that there are even unwritten "traffic laws" for how to walk on the sidewalk, and you may feel the ire of the locals if you violate them. Structures and expectations are grease on the wheels of social life.

What happens when these rules and structures go too far? That is, what happens when rules and structures stifle the freedom of individuals to live authentically? An example of this kind of structural overreach was the "Don't ask, don't tell" policy implemented in the United States military in the 1990s. At that time, the policy stated that LGBT individuals could serve only if their sexual orientation remained a secret.

If anyone else in the armed services learned of their sexuality, they were required to report it, and the individual was discharged from their service. This policy, which was intended to create a way for LGBT individuals to serve in the military, forced them to conceal a core part of their identities (including, for instance, being unable to talk about their spouses or domestic partners with others).

A more recent example happened when the onset of the COVID-19 pandemic in 2020 led to the swift implementation of a wide range of lockdowns and restrictions around the world. The rules were enacted with the goal of reducing the spread and minimizing the impact of the virus, with a particular sensitivity to the possibility of overwhelming healthcare systems. And while most people could agree on the goals of the restrictions, the reality is that they had a vastly differential impact on people depending on their circumstances. For instance, individuals whose jobs could be done remotely or whose salaries were relatively secure had a very different experience from those whose wages depended on showing up in person somewhere, especially when the business or organization was forced to close for an indefinite amount of time, or for gig workers whose gigs suddenly evaporated. And, perhaps not surprisingly, these distinctions tended to break down along existing lines of inequality, such that individuals who already were sitting in a precarious situation economically were disproportionately strained by the restrictions. In a way, it was inevitable that the restrictions would become politicized and lead to protests.

What happens in situations like these? How is it that the need for structure and predictability goes too far, and how can it be resolved? The lesson of Mercury is not to do away with the rules and structures—that is, to dissolve into anarchy. As we've seen, the child needs the rules and structures to provide boundary conditions, and with an understanding of the limits they are free to act within those limits. Relating the child's experience back to the situations above, what we can see is that rather than focusing on a shared understanding of the objectives and allowing for creativity in the pursuit of those objectives, the process was reversed: the behaviors were prescribed (or proscribed), and any deviation from or challenge to those set behaviors was interpreted as antithetical to the goal. In other words, the behavior stood as a proxy for the goal, leaving no freedom in the realm of action without risking stigma or ostracism.

In psychology, there is a phenomenon known as *reactance* that emerges when someone feels that their autonomy is being threatened, and in social life we see it awaken whenever there is talk of making something mandatory or forbidden. Research in this area finds that when reactance is triggered, individuals can experience anger and hostility, and they increase the value placed on the forbidden option and downgrade their preference for the imposed option. Politicians are masters of manipulating this experience, often portraying the opposing side as trying to impose their way or limit people's freedom. True or false, it has the desired effect of deepening entrenchment and polarization.

In such situations, Mercury wants to have clarity in structure *and* freedom in action. Clarity in structure comes from identifying the shared goal or objective—what is it we're trying to do here? Finding a shared goal may not be a trivial step; it may require real communication and dialogue to establish a shared sense of the big picture. An important aspect here is the sincere belief in the good faith of everyone involved, which includes accepting their concerns and perspectives as *true for them*. There is an adage that says that only when you can articulate someone else's position in a way that they find acceptable are you ready to begin the conversation. Once a shared understanding of the goals and concerns is reached, then the possibility opens up for individuals to pursue those goals in ways that fit their unique strengths and circumstances. Of course, there still needs to be room for external inputs about which strategies might be more or less effective, but individuals will likely remain more open to those inputs because their autonomy does not feel threatened. The expression "all roads lead to Rome" captures this notion that there is more than one way to reach the same goal.

The previous examples were huge and heavy issues, but we can apply this basic principle to many everyday situations. A great example that has received attention recently has to do with how teachers greet their students in the morning. In the past, teachers might have had a single way of greeting students, such as a handshake. However, with the increase in cultural diversity in classrooms and the awareness that students differ in their sensitivity to physical contact, there was an opportunity to reassess. What is the real purpose of the greeting? If it is to create a moment of one-on-one connection with each student, then there are many paths to this goal. Some teachers have started putting up greeting charts at their classroom doors, and each child indicates whether they want a handshake or a high-five or a wave or a hug. Here we see the impulse of Mercury at work, allowing for freedom within form and keeping a mundane situation from ever becoming entirely predictable.

In one final connection to this theme, we can see in the previous example a distinction between *equity* and *equality*, which are major components of contemporary conversations about diversity and inclusion. To put the distinction very crudely, equality says that everyone gets the same, whereas equity says that everyone gets what they need. To illustrate the distinction, a different teacher who becomes aware that not everyone is comfortable with physical touch could implement an equality approach to the morning greeting—for instance, the handshake is replaced by a wave. In this approach, one mandate is replaced by another, and the need that the teacher is aware of (sensitivity to touch) is prioritized over other needs that they may be unaware of, such as the fact that in certain cultures waving is considered offensive. The equity approach, in contrast, allows each child to choose their own way to serve the goal of connection without having to articulate the reasons for their preferences. It trusts individuals to know best what they need and to pursue that path without stigma.

Qualities of Mercury

Mercury embodies the principle of motion like no other planet. As the planet closest to the Sun, it has the shortest orbital period of just 88 days. Due to its elliptical orbit, it moves more slowly when it is farther from the Sun, creating an unsteadiness in its speed. A Mercury year is short; however, a Mercury day, from sunrise to sunset, is almost endlessly long at 58 Earth days. This is only topped by Venus, whose day lasts 116 Earth days. The porous, rocky planet strewn with craters is exposed to extreme temperature fluctuations. Temperatures reach up to 430°C (806°F) on the sunny side due to the proximity to the Sun and -173°C (-279°F) on the side facing away from the Sun. Another distinctive feature of Mercury is that its rotational axis is almost perfectly upright. It doesn't lean one way or another or "wobble" like the Earth does as it orbits the Sun. Symbolically, we could say this uprightness is related to having no preconceptions or preset plans that lean in one direction or another, so in this position of uprightness Mercury is ready to move in any direction at any time. So we see the planet Mercury is the great uniter of opposites that remains open to all possibilities.

The planet Mercury also exhibits restlessness. It can be seen at dawn and dusk, but not always equally well. For a long time, astronomers had difficulty calculating its orbit. In 1543, Copernicus wrote about this challenge in *De Revolutionibus*: "[T]he planet has made us take many detours and undergo much labour in order to examine its wanderings."[30] With all the data from his predecessor, sixteenth-century Danish astronomer Tycho Brahe, the seventeenth-century German astronomer Johannes Kepler was able to predict a so-called Mercury transit of the Sun for November 7, 1631, for the first time. Although Kepler died before the event, French philosopher Pierre Gassendi managed to observe the predicted passage in front of the Sun. However, he almost missed it because at that time it was assumed that the size of Mercury was much larger than its true size, and he just caught sight of a small black point moving across the Sun. Here the transformation and the play of the forces of Mercury come to light. One assumes, of course, that it is big, and then there is a restless little point that chases the Sun. Here, too, it unites opposites.

The metal associated with Mercury is, not surprisingly, mercury or quicksilver. Here again we see a repetition of the qualities of mobility, deception, and uniting opposites. For instance, mercury is the only metal that is liquid at room temperature, and, historically, this fact made it useful in applications like thermometers and barometers, and even in fluorescent light bulbs. It is a miracle of nature that mercury is liquid at all, as it is twice as dense as iron and fourteen times heavier than water! So it connects heaviness and easy mobility. This liquid mercury unites another opposite property: If mercury encounters resistance, it bursts into innumerable small drops . . . but if the small drops come into the slightest contact with one another, they immediately recombine. Its cohesive power is tremendously strong. So it unites the opposites of dissolution and unification. In nature, mercury can be found in the form of the ore cinnabar, which means "dragon's blood" because it shows up in fiery red cinnabar crystals. Here, too, mercury plays a deception, because it sheds the metallic element and shows itself in the garb of a semiprecious stone.

A person with a lot of Mercury qualities is a light-footed, lively person, a master of transformation and disguise—think Robin Williams or Jim Carrey—who can embody an entirely new persona from one moment to the next. Or consider a door-to-door salesman, whose effervescent demeanor and gift of gab have you committing to a new mattress topper before you realize you don't need one. By the time you come to, he's already working on his next sale across town. The contrast here is between the warmth and interest of the sales pitch and the abrupt disappearance after the deal.

It is easy to get out of breath when dealing with the quick pace and fluid nature of Mercury, and yet the lungs are actually the organ that goes along with Mercury. The lungs are a place of mystery and transformation where inner becomes outer and vice versa. The natural state of the lungs, like Mercury, is movement. It becomes apparent whenever we try to hold our breath that our lungs want to be breathing. Interestingly, mercury the metal also exhibits a kind of breathing process. Mercury at room temperature is indifferent toward oxygen, but if you heat it close to its boiling point, then the "interest" in oxygen is aroused. The oxygen reacts with mercury to create a reddish powder known as mercury oxide. But if you continue to heat it, this oxygen is released again. So you could say that, depending on the degree of heat, the mercury breathes in or out, like a small metal lung.

Both the planet and metal are named after the god Mercury from Roman mythology. Many of the stories and symbols associated with

Mercury are derived from the Greek god Hermes, with whom he shares many features, and there is speculation that Hermes also may have been derived from (or morphed with) the Egyptian god Thoth. Thoth—who is often depicted as a man with the head of an ibis bird—stood with Anubis at the gates of the underworld, where the deceased's heart was weighed against the Feather of Truth to determine their worthiness for the afterlife. His role was scribe, and as such, he recorded the outcomes of these trials—in fact, it has been said that he was the one who created hieroglyphics, along with a number of other branches of knowledge, including law and medicine. Justice and fairness were his hallmarks, just as the planet Mercury stands upright in its axis. He presided over the battle between Horus and Set, where he stopped the battle several times in order to heal one or the other combatant to ensure a fair fight. In the underworld, he accompanied souls on their journeys, and used magic spells to protect and revive them.

Stories depict Hermes (and his Roman counterpart, Mercury) as the messenger of the gods. Hermes/Mercury is most recognizable by his winged sandals and hat, and he carries the caduceus—a winged staff with two snakes wrapped around it. Fleet-footed and clever, Hermes/Mercury could often be found playing tricks on others, sometimes for good and sometimes for fun. He was particularly fond of finding clever ways to steal things that belonged to the other gods, and is, in fact, the patron of thieves, in addition to his associations with commerce, travel, and communication. In each persona, we can see these qualities of exchange or "going between." He was also an inventor, creating the first lyre from a tortoise shell (which he gave to Apollo to make up for a trick he had played) and the panpipes, a type of flute. Like Thoth, he was credited with inventing writing, and he guided souls to the river Styx in the underworld, where they would be ferried to Hades and meet their judgment. Thus, across all of these mythological representations, Hermes/Mercury is characterized as a clever trickster, a messenger and go-between, a traveling companion, a healer, and an inventor.

Working with Mercury Forces in Daily Life: Riding the Wave

You're in a hurry, you're running late, and the children are dawdling. You announce that everyone should please come to the table now for breakfast, but this command fails to work, and they happily dawdle on. There are more admonitions, threats, and shouting. In the end, everyone is annoyed, and somehow you make it to their school on time.

The whole rigmarole is repeated the next day. The rush meets dawdling, threats fall on deaf ears, and the screaming finally drives the children on to school, where you expect them to start their lessons calmly and with concentration. And the day after? You guessed it, it continues in the same way. "Insanity is doing the same thing over and over again and expecting different results." [Note: This quote is often attributed to Albert Einstein, but, in a Mercurial twist, there is no record of Einstein ever speaking or writing this line. Whoever is responsible for inventing this statement, the point remains.]

Our example of repetitive morning chaos shows a situation that is difficult to break through. Just as we spoke of *scripted fun* at the beginning, we now confront the already-know-how-it-will-go spiral. Not planned, but completely predictable. You follow the same recipe and somehow expect a different cake, and one hectic morning predictably follows the other.

In the wonderful film *Groundhog Day*, Phil Connors (played by Bill Murray) wakes up every morning on the same day for a seemingly endless number of times. He cannot break out of this cycle despite his best efforts. Only when he steps out of his own tunnel vision, commits himself to helping others, and fully engages in connecting with his colleague Rita (played by Andie MacDowell) does he succeed.

This is where the power of riding the wave lies. In a situation that has become stagnant, you pause, look for an approaching wave, connect with it mercurially, and suddenly the situation can flow again. The example of the children dawdling in the morning could look like this: "Ah, one of them is having trouble getting dressed, the other is playing, the third is reading a book. Obviously, they are all just oblivious to what time it is." You could stand up and call out, "Whoever sits first at the breakfast table wins: Ready, set, go!" Or another time you could start singing a funny song, first softly until someone sings along and then louder and louder until everyone does their tasks while singing. (There were five children in Anne's family growing up, and when it was too loud and hectic at the dining table, her father would sometimes say: "Whoever can scream the loudest wins!" So they would all shout as loudly as possible, and after that there was silence.)

Riding the wave is a skill that can be acquired well with the help of humor, as illustrated by another example: One day, a child declares that he can no longer do his math homework. It's too hard. Yesterday he could solve these problems with ease, but not today. "There's no use trying—I just can't do it!" The parent rebuts: "You could do it yesterday, so quit whining and just do it!" How will the child react? A) "You know what, you're right, I was able to do that yesterday. Thank you, I'll do it right away!" or B) "I DON'T KNOW HOW TO DO IT! I CANNOT DO THIS!" and a lot of tortured time goes by before the homework is finally done. B is so predictable! And A? If we're honest, it's unthinkable!

However, if we ride the wave that the situation offers, it might go like this: "I cannot do this!" "Oh, really? Show me what you've got there. . . . Yes, those really do look like tough problems. Maybe impossible." What will the reaction be then? A) "No I can't!" or B) "I bet you I can figure them out. I'm going to try again!" The mercurial riding of the wave brought movement into the situation again, through a deep, immediate connection with what revealed itself, then the dissolution, and everyone returns to their tasks. Every wave is different, so you can never plan your response in advance; here, Mercury demands incredible mobility without losing yourself. The heaviness of the metal helps with this "staying grounded."

Perhaps one last example comes from the other side of the wave. Imagine that you are in the fitting room trying on a summer dress. It almost fits well, but not quite, and the color is rather unusual for you. You're not sure if this is a good choice, so you ask the saleswoman. She says: "Oh, that suits you perfectly!" You reply: "Really? Don't you think the fit makes me look a bit frumpy? And doesn't the color make me look a little pale?" "No, no, it looks great!" What do you do? You take it off and leave the store. Another salesperson who knows how to ride the waves would say: "What do you think? Is it comfortable? Do you wear this color often?" Upon revealing your uncertainty, she would say: "Wait a minute, I think I have something that will suit you better." She has caught your wave, and you will wait to see what she brings you. When someone catches your wave, you feel picked up, noticed, seen, and appreciated, and that's a good, magical momentum to feel.

A Good Laugh and a Good Cry

Have you ever laughed yourself to tears? Or cried until your sobs morphed into uncontrollable laughter? How can two expressions at opposite ends of the emotional spectrum be so closely connected? Perhaps Mercury can help us see laughter and weeping in a new light and add to our toolbox for getting ourselves (and others) unstuck.

Of all our emotional expressions, laughter and weeping are most closely connected to the breath, giving them a mercurial quality. With laughter, deep inhalations are paired with staccato exhalations, while the opposite is true with weeping. Karl König, Austrian pediatrician and founder of the Camphill Movement, suggested that laughter and weeping are "guardians who stand at two different gates," helping us maintain a right relationship between our inner and outer worlds.[31] He also said that both hold the potential to bring healing or restore equilibrium: "A disturbance in our relationship to the world is cause for weeping and laughing. . . . They are like remedies; they restore a condition which has lost its proportions."[32]

We are all familiar with the expressions "a good cry" and "a good laugh," and we can recognize these experiences by the feeling of calmness and relief that comes in their wake. We feel somehow nourished. Yet, for most people a good laugh or cry is not an everyday occurrence. Why not? For one thing, they both carry a certain social stigma. To laugh or cry uncontrollably in a board meeting or in the grocery store or in the park would attract attention and probably spark concerns about your mental health. You can almost hear someone saying, "What's wrong with you? Get a hold of yourself!" Under ordinary circumstances, most of us are adept at holding back our propensity to laugh or cry or at least modulating our expressions. Instead, we translate our feelings into calmly expressed words—"Oh, that's so sad!" or "Hahaha . . . That's so funny!" Research shows that the common, more controlled social laugh is distinct from its more involuntary cousin, including being associated with the activation of different brain regions.[33] In contrast, in moments when we break into uncontrollable laughter or tears, the force of the situation has overwhelmed us. The times when we willingly give ourselves over to laughter or tears—have a good laugh or a good cry—are typically private situations where we are by ourselves or with safe company, like our spouses or best friends.

If we transport ourselves back to our childhoods, however, we'd find a different situation. Children have very little power or interest in holding back their laughter or tears. And although as parents we sometimes wish they'd dial it back a little, we nonetheless feel pure vitality in these expressions. They are entering fully into their experience and allowing themselves to be moved by it. We see this less and less as children move toward adolescence, no doubt in part because they learn what kind of behavior is valued by parents and teachers. It's another aspect of childhood that gets squeezed out in the service of maturity. And just like the kind of scripted fun we discussed earlier, society creates structured opportunities for feeling and expressing these feelings in a socially sanctioned way. For instance, the entertainment industry creates films that are meant to evoke laughter and tears (among other emotions, like fear), and they kindly turn down the lights so we don't need to feel self-conscious.

What would happen if we could reconnect with our capacity to express ourselves in this way? How would the tone of social situations be changed if we started bringing little bits of Mercury in—if we really laughed instead of saying something was funny, or if we allowed tears to come to our eyes when something sad happens? Drawing on earlier lessons, we'd have to start from the premise that failure is possible, and that that's okay. It could be met with stony silence, or with others walking away. But also remember that drops of Mercury attach easily to one another and draw others toward them. When one person takes a chance, it opens the door to others doing the same, and soon the whole tone of the situation can become more humanized. Deep down, many of us long to reconnect with the carefree childlike parts of ourselves. We're just waiting for permission to lay down our armor.

The Just-Because Impulse

Those who act out of an impulse often encounter headshaking. There are some impulses that don't have a good reputation in polite society. Revving your engine in the city center at 1:00 a.m., for example, does not endear you to sleeping residents. But there is definitely an age where impulses are the driving force to conquer the powers of the imagination and also learning strategies—the period of middle childhood. Great feelings are given unbridled expression. Any perceived injustice is met with theatrical lamentations and deep expressions of bafflement. Even unstoppable guffaws of laughter can fill the room. If we as parents stop the child and ask why they are acting this way, we may get a simple response—"Just because." And just as these impulses find expression, they also suddenly fizzle out again. Since the possibility of failure at this age is of great importance in learning to learn, the impulses are free of expectations and goals. But the unrestrained expression does not go hand in hand with the absence of boundaries. As we mentioned earlier, it's all about freedom within form.

When do we lose this creative impulsivity in the course of life, and why? When, as adults, we indulge our impulses, things often look quite different. Who, for instance, hasn't ordered a piece of cake for dessert out of an impulse even though they were actually already full? Or bought a trendy blouse that caught their eye on a sunny day in spring? And who hasn't later regretted such an impulsive act? You felt a little sick after the piece of cake, and the trendy blouse still hangs in your closet with the tags attached! Or maybe you've acted on an impulse to get up and leave a situation where you were feeling stuck. That can definitely be a good thing and set the necessary changes in motion, but it's not the same as the carefree, playful impulsivity of the child.

The key is in the why. The mercurial just-because impulse is devoid of expectations and goals; it serves solely as a breeding ground for the joys in life. These impulses are small invitations that appear on the edge of the path of life and may be accepted or not. They bring color and little stories to everyday life, which sometimes tends to become a little gray and dull. Since they are free of anything binding, there is usually no remorse when accepting the invitation. They are fluid moments of joy.

An example can shed some light on this mystery of little happiness: Imagine you have an appointment in town at 7:00 p.m., and by 6:00 p.m. you have finished all of your tasks. You could find something to fill that time—maybe do some cleaning, write a grocery list, or research options for an upcoming vacation. If you did any of those things, you might feel as if you were *extra* productive. Or maybe instead you recognize that it takes about an hour to walk from home to town—a beautiful path over fields, streets, and nice rows of old town houses—and you just start walking. No reason—just because—period. If you start thinking about how walking to town will gain you 6,000 steps and burn 250 calories, you've lost the Mercury moment. The next thing you know you're searching drawers for your pedometer and googling how many calories are in a beer to see if you'd "earn" one on your walk. Can you see the shift? All sorts of things start creeping into the moment of happiness and wipe away the joy.

Here's another example: Anne met some people from Finland at a conference several years ago. She began to get to know them, and they quickly became warm friends—later, she even went to visit them in their home country. Some time after that, she learned about a system for learning any language with ease, and she thought: Why not give Finnish a try? Did she need to learn it? No, all of her Finnish friends spoke English. Was she interested in learning another language? Not particularly. Is it an easy language to learn? On the contrary, it's considered one of the more difficult languages to pick up. So why might she go for it? Just the simple joy of trying. Today, she continues to enthusiastically work to improve, and she even gave a speech in Finnish at a recent conference in Finland. It's not tied to an end goal, and there are no rewards—she just does it for the sheer joy.

Just-because impulses are tailor-made and are individual invitations to enrich your own life. Few of us would ever throw ourselves off a bridge with a bungee cord on our legs, though this opportunity might present itself sometime. We could say no, thank you, and move on, satisfied, feeling no regrets for a missed opportunity. The just-because impulse is more about noticing the flowers along the path than about planning a trip to a botanical garden. The path, not the goal, is what is important.

> Where do you find refreshing moments of "just because" in your life? What are some ways you can reconnect to the free, childlike part of yourself in your daily activities?

Catch Me(rcury) if You Can

Let's try again to grasp the entire field of activity of Mercury: Mercury is recognized by its evanescence, its strong cohesion, and its capacity for dispersion. It may be easy to forget the mercurial qualities from daily life because they are so fleeting. It is also possible that in the Mercury years in particular, if our parents or teachers did not appreciate our playful, mercurial nature, we may have curbed it in order not to disappoint others. As volatile as the metal is, the soul qualities can be just as easily wiped away. A critical glance is enough, and whoosh, the impulse is gone. But it is precisely this lightness that we need to invite in and enjoy! Don't you feel refreshed, even renewed, after an unexpected bout of laughter? Don't we all long for moments of liberated lightness every now and then? Mercury whispers this longingly in your ear so it is not forgotten.

Mercury is not a rhythmic being in the sense that you can guess the next beat, and yet it is not purely coincidental. Instead, it invites you to sharpen your senses to recognize its invitations on the wayside of life. You can awaken just-because impulses and let them add a little syncopation to the rhythm of life—a little rhythmic refreshment or revitalization. One route to tapping into your inner Mercury is to open yourself to the liberating and healing effects of humor. Crack a childish joke, laugh until your ribs hurt, notice the little absurdities that life serves you. You don't have to be afraid of appearing ridiculous because Mercury lives purely in the present moment. It does not express guilt and does not allow remorse. And while you're at it, pull someone into your moment of humor, then let them go again. Encounter and movement—binding and loosening. Let Mercury interrupt the predictable flow of everyday life in a cheerful, healing, flowing, fleeting manner. Just because!

3

VENUS

Who Do You Think I Am?

THE NOTION THAT AGING CAN BE STOPPED OR REVERSED HAS captivated the human imagination throughout history. The epic of Gilgamesh, written up to four thousand years ago, describes a plant at the bottom of the sea that can restore Gilgamesh's youth and provide immortality. He finds the plant, but then loses it to a snake before he can test its power. In alchemy, the Philosopher's Stone—also known as the elixir of life—was purported to have the power to heal and prolong life. And explorers like Juan Ponce de León crossed oceans in search of the Fountain of Youth. Although we may believe ourselves to be much more sensible these days, there is no end to the demand for face creams, dietary supplements, injections, hair dyes, compression clothing, or cosmetic surgeries to help us resist aging, at least in appearances.

Why are we so endlessly fascinated by the idea of holding onto our youth? Perhaps we have the idea that the apex of physical attractiveness occurs in youth—before gravity sets in and we become decorated with wrinkles and grey hairs. It is, to be sure, a time of great vitality, but is it really the peak of beauty? The media and advertising agencies would surely like us to think so, and they have centuries of art history behind them. We hardly bat an eye encountering a painting or sculpture of a youthful nude at an art museum, but a middle-aged or elder nude would surely turn heads away. And in the age of airbrushing and digital manipulation, even portrayals of young people in the media are "touched up" to push them further from reality toward the "ideal." We may know at some level that we cannot *actually* become young again, but we may long to be seen like we were when we were young.

Or maybe we look back at our youth as a time of fun, excitement, and limited responsibility. We remember hanging out with our friends all the time, listening to music, playing sports, watching movies. No bills to pay, no rent, no kids to be responsible for, no bosses to appease . . . how great it would be to return to those days! Actually, a moment's reflection likely reveals that this memory is more than a little idealistic. Not only were there a lot of things that were hard about being young, but we can also likely point to a number of important lessons we've learned about ourselves and life since then that we wouldn't want to unlearn. Okay, so maybe we can go back to the youthful look, but can we keep all of the life lessons? Perhaps this isn't ideal either; while young people might attract attention because of their outward beauty, that superficial look may come along with a presumption of a lack of inner depth. When was the last time you turned to a teenager for advice (except maybe to understand the finer points of TikTok etiquette)?

The power of Venus comes through forming a personal relationship with the idea of beauty. It's about embracing ourselves as we are ("Warts and all," as is said), connecting with the idea that who we are is beautiful even if it isn't always pretty, and radiating outward this sense of inner beauty to warm the spaces we enter.

> If you could choose one age to look like, one age to feel like, and one age to think like, which ages would you choose? Would any of them be the same, or even match your current age?

Under Construction: Enter at Your Own Risk

Suddenly you wake up from a soft dream and stand face-to-face with the cold, harsh world. You wonder how you could have been sitting around playing with dolls your whole life when there is so much injustice in the world. Nothing fits together anymore, from your suddenly elongated limbs to the incredibly hollow ideas and views of your parents. An abyss of feelings opens up, and many adolescents get pulled into a vortex. A sign goes up on the bedroom door: "Under Construction: Enter at Your Own Risk!" Even as a parent you can look across the dining table at the person sitting where your little child used to sit and think, *Who are you? Where has my sweet daughter gone? My courteous son?* What is astonishing here is that the adults, who have all pressed themselves through the same eye of the needle, can still be amazed and upset at this sight instead of looking at their offspring with great compassion and interest.

We know that a major renovation is actually taking place, triggered by the onset of sexual maturity. The child's body begins to stretch seemingly uncontrolled in all directions, their skin becomes oily, body hair begins to sprout, and their voice starts to break. The worst part is, we also know that from now on everything about the growing child will be judged mercilessly by themselves and others. What will count is what is on the billboards, and those who can't achieve it—the six-pack, the feminine curves, the full lips, and so on—will feel like a failure. It may seem like someone pulled the rug out from under them, and they find themselves in a free fall. But we know it's a construction site, that there is chaos, and nothing looks the way the architect thought it would—at least not yet. The ideal is made abundantly clear, but the way to get there isn't going to be pretty. Can you remember how it felt when nobody understood you, and you couldn't find any space to work it out on your own? When your mother stood in the doorway nagging you about the chaos in your room? You would like to have said, "Sorry Mom, but I really have bigger problems I need to work through right now!" but the words came out as, "Leave me alone!"

We may also remember that during these years, it wasn't easy to find the right words, especially around adults. You might have had so much to say but no idea how to say it. Even extremely talkative children can fall into a strangely loud silence on entering puberty. On the flip side, young people can develop their own language to communicate with their peers. Haven't we all sat on the bus in amazement, listening to the boys talking and marveling at the words they were using? Their language may also be peppered with profanity and insults, but none of them seem to be offended. You wonder how they could be communicating anything at all with their words, but they clearly understand each other.

To better understand the peculiarities of this youth language, it can help to rewatch a movie that was popular when you were young. *Easy Rider, Saturday Night Fever, The Breakfast Club, Mall Rats*—every generation has something that can transport them back to those years. Maybe you've even tried to create a special bonding moment by watching one of these films with your teenagers. But as you hit play on these favorites as an adult, you might find yourself sinking into the sofa, embarrassed that the language you connected with so strongly back then now sounds like words from another planet. You can't bear to glance over at your teenagers and risk catching one of their eye rolls. You wonder what happened.

This youth language, with its newly created words and phrases, is an extremely interesting phenomenon. At the most basic level, language has to be renewed again and again in order to bring new ideas into social life. For instance, words like "cryptocurrency" and "cybersecurity" had no reason to exist before the proliferation of computers and the internet. But language can also be generated to create new meaning for something that already exists. The experience of sexual objectification and coercion in the workplace sadly has a long history, particularly for women, but historically it was considered just part of the job. When the term "sexual harassment" was created in the 1970s, it provided a new lens for this old phenomenon and set into motion social, political, and legal campaigns that empowered individuals to demand better treatment at work. And although these language innovations were not created by the youth, the generative and audacious language of the youth is a training ground for them. Just as Mercury and the middle childhood years are linked to the present, Venus and this age of adolescence are linked to the forces of the future. So it's worth listening with interest to the young people and simply letting their language unfold.

Let's go past the bedroom door again, behind which a teenager has been holed up for weeks. The only sign of life coming from within is the occasional change in the music that can be heard halfway down the block. We only see him now and then, shuffling home from school or sitting at the dining table, his hoodie pulled low over his forehead. A mumbled "Hello" is his highest form of communication. Take a closer look at the sign on the door: Under Construction—Enter at Your Own Risk!

What does this sign really mean? We feel it as a gesture of pushing us away, but it doesn't say, "Go away!" Perhaps it's actually an invitation: "I dare you to come in, wade through the outer and inner chaos, and really see me." The adolescent really is a construction site, most noticeably in the physical realm. Anne recalls one year when her son needed new shoes every two months because his feet were growing so quickly. It was annoying because it became very expensive, but what could her son do about it? Nothing, it was what it was. You can't be angry at growing feet, right?

But of course their minds and emotional lives are transforming as much as their bodies, and it makes just as little sense to get angry about rapidly growing ideas or emotions. The *feeling life* in particular is a real hotspot of the renovation. Sensations, desires, sympathy, and antipathy forces stir like a storm. As much as adolescents have difficulty recognizing themselves through all of these changes, it's doubly disorienting when those who've known them for the longest—their parents—seem to lose their connection to the future butterfly who is currently in a state of mush inside the cocoon.

One area where the feeling life gets outwardly activated during this time is in the search for ideals and idols. Adolescents look up to great personalities who know what they're doing; they aspire to have such charisma. Movie stars, athletes, musicians, even leaders of social movements can attract the interest of adolescents. Those with a strong voice, a clear sense of who they are, and a worthwhile purpose are particularly magnetic. And while some of these purposes may be nobler than others (e.g., solving the climate crisis vs. driving a sports car), they point to a newfound fire in the adolescent that is searching for the right direction to be channeled into.

On the other hand, there is a risk of selfishness and overindulgence during these years, including an increased likelihood of risky and addictive behaviors. The prevention expert Felicitas Vogt defines addiction as an act of substitution for the higher self or "I." Behind the addiction lies the longing for self-efficacy and self-development, but the feeling that we cannot meet the ideals and expectations we see in the world creates an opening for these addictive behaviors to stand between ourselves and these goals.

So it is an extremely fragile time—despite the hardness and the need for absolutes that the young people project into the world. The self-discovery process opens up on a *still missing* life story. The question, "Who am I?" can only be endured, because there is not yet any basis for answering it. You could say that this newly opened inner world must first be explored with a blindfold. One can only *feel* one's way around, and it is precisely at the obstacles and hurdles that one gradually awakens to this inner landscape.

So, what can adults do to accompany this process with the necessary care? Parents can first build a mood of trust and an open attitude with invisible safety nets. It is important for the adolescent to practice stepping out on the tightrope of life and taking a chance, and it is equally important for their inevitable falls to become opportunities for learning rather than catastrophes. To support this gesture, it helps for parents to move from the role of authority to the role of a personality. You can get involved in political discussions with young people not to belittle them or prove them wrong, but to create an opportunity for them to try on different ideas, challenge themselves, and sharpen their knives. The subject teacher at school who is a master on his subject and who understands his craft to a high degree will encourage students to develop mastery themselves; a teacher who does not, will immediately lose the students' respect.

In summary, it is safe to say that during adolescence, an inner fragility is often compensated for with an outer hardness. Adolescents want to be able to compete and assert themselves in real encounters, yet at the same time they withdraw and seek like-minded people. They develop their own language to connect and express themselves to "their people" and create some distance from everyone else. As an adult onlooker, it will help if, now and then, you can try to see the opposite of what is thrown at you as true. "You just don't understand me!" could mean, "I don't understand myself. I still love you, but I need to figure this out on my own. Please stay close and be available when I come looking for you."

Think back to your teenage years. Who were the idols, heroes, or personalities you looked up to? What captivated you about them? Can you see a lasting influence of these individuals on your life?

The Catwalk of Life

When was the last time you had tears in your eyes because you were overwhelmed by the beauty of a person, a sunset, a piece of music, or a work of art? What went through your mind and body when you found your dream wedding dress? What is this irrepressible power of beauty that can dissolve time and space for a moment, enveloping you also in feeling what was good and true at the same time? Is that how you feel when you take one last look in the mirror before leaving the house in the morning? If not, what is different?

This trinity consisting of goodness, truth, and beauty has been discussed since at least Plato's time. Are these goals to be achieved or rather are they lighthouses that point in the direction of the ideal? Let's go back briefly to a moment in your past where you were overwhelmed by all three. For example, perhaps you were sitting in a concert hall when the pianist struck the first notes of Chopin's "Nocturne 1," and you could feel in your body that the sound was good, true, and beautiful! You didn't need to say anything about it, and if you tried, your words would have failed you. The experience spoke for itself.

But what about the beauty in everyday life? In our times, beauty has been degraded from a higher (even spiritual) ideal to a billion-dollar industry. The magazine rack at the supermarket presents a unified vision of what beauty means: white teeth, slim legs, no wrinkles, well-toned bodies, and relaxed parents with happy young children. We know, or we think we know at least, what other people consider beautiful, and we do our best to conform. In doing so, we unwittingly reinforce the idea that we, too, find beauty in this way. As an adult this might not be all too damaging, but where beauty can be grasped or conceived individually for the first time—in adolescence—it is far more complicated. Adolescents just don't know who they are, what kind of beauty has been given to them through grace. And what rounds off the whole catastrophe is that society offers these wonderful, colorful, agile, and curious young people an unspeakably unimaginative, dull, and boring broth of the ordinary as the ideal of the beautiful.

The catwalk serves as the highest platform in the fashion industry. What appears there determines the colors of spring, whether tight or loose trousers are "in," and when it's safe to revive the shoulder pads and animal prints. Every day as we step out onto the catwalk of life, we're put to the test of just how clued in we are to these shifting ideas. With age you can become a little more resistant to the annual requirements, but for the high school student, staying up-to-date can be seen as a matter of survival. Should they wear that sweater from last winter that they love so much? A friend says, "I wouldn't be caught dead in that." And the sweater makes its way to the donation bin. Can we see anything good, true, and beautiful in this situation? Is true beauty subject to impermanence? Isn't it about time to release children from this nonsense?

From an early age, one of Anne's daughters has had an unusual relationship with colors, patterns, and their combinations when it comes to clothes. Often she would come out of her room with the question: "And? How do you like this?" Anne would sometimes respond with a smile: "It makes my eyes hurt!" Whereupon her daughter would say, "I like it," and then she started to glow. Anne couldn't help but see her true, good beauty, and whenever it happened, she was moved by what was happening before her eyes. Her daughter's choice of clothes would never reach the cover of a fashion magazine, but it always took Anne's heart by storm. This example shows how kindling an inner knowing of beauty can bolster young people's resilience to the onslaught of images they face from the outside. Not feeling the need to constantly cross-check their appearance with their new style can free up inner resources that support their development. And as they step out into the world on their own and are "seen" more and more by others, they can experience the burst of self-confidence that comes from being comfortable in their own skin.

I'm Speechless

How do we reconcile the linguistic creativity that arises out of every generation of youth with the fact that they struggle to find the words to communicate with adults? In a way, the situation bears similarity to one where an individual is trying to communicate in a non-native language: while they may speak effortlessly in their native tongue, their speech is necessarily simplified when trying to say something in a language they have only a basic grasp of. Such challenges of communication have sometimes sparked the question of whether a universal language could be created that all people speak and communicate effectively with, such as Esperanto. In an essay, the Czech-Brazilian media philosopher and communication scientist Vilém Flusser (1920–1991) developed an interesting thought on this possibility. In it he says: "Assuming that everyone speaks the same language everywhere . . . would assume that they had nothing new to say to each other. Because wherever something is said that has not been said before, either the vocabulary changes (new words are created) or the syntax (new language rules arise) or both. The universal language would break down into sub-languages."[34]

In other words, a universal language cannot last because new language is needed to capture new experiences, which are necessarily different in different parts of the world. It follows that the same must be true within a society or even within families. There, too, new things happen that must be put into words. Language is never complete—it is eternally evolving. This is what every generation of youth struggles with in its time. They bring a new impulse to an outdated system. If you approach them with: "We've always done it this way!" or "Why are you talking that way?!" they are held back in their art of expression. Instead, we can approach the language of the youth from the other direction: "What actually wants to develop in the world that needs this new language to outgrow speechlessness?" Once more, let's turn this over to Vilém Flusser, who said:

According to this [idea], national languages (and all sub-languages in general) are tools for creating the NEW, also creative instruments. They are all, without exception, great products of the human will to generate something new. All languages, without exception, are triumphs of the spirit in its struggle against the stubbornness of the world into which we have been thrown, and each language has a beauty of its own that cannot be found anywhere else. So if you love your own language, you love everyone else's, because only in comparison to others does the beauty of your own language and the other shine."[35]

Isn't that a surprise? We encounter the beauty of our own language when dealing with strangers. And our own children, as adolescents, can sometimes seem like strangers who challenge us to reconnect with our language. When we are working with the same old ideas and words, language is easy, but the beauty of language becomes visible on the frictional surfaces of diversity. If we only move among our own kind, then this awareness of the beauty of language remains hidden from us.

Let's go back to the time of word creation. We mentioned how young people are connected to the future. The language arriving from the future is one that brings new things into the world for which there are no terms yet. Providing adolescents with a family council platform, like a round table, where ideas can be discussed back and forth without concern about correctness, morality, or anything else, can be helpful. Anne's family worked with a family council process like this. At these round-table meetings, everyone could equally say what they had to say. They could look at tricky family issues from all sides and find unusual solutions in the interplay that somehow satisfied everyone, but which could never have been devised by the parents alone. A creative language culture in the family helps strengthen individual freedom and starts to pave a path of peace.

Big words never come out as trite phrases. Let's look at politicians, a group that is caught in a language inhibition and politicizes issues by repeating the same "talking points" over and over. It takes a courageous person like Nelson Mandela or Martin Luther King to bring new thoughts into the world using new words. You can read their speeches or writings many times and always discover something new in them. The language of poetry can also help here to put the inexpressible into words. With that in mind, let's close this section with a little poem by Emily Dickinson:[36]

> *I died for Beauty, but was scarce*
> *Adjusted in the tomb,*
> *When one who died for truth was lain*
> *In an adjoining room.*

He questioned softly why I failed?
"For beauty," I replied.
"And I for truth, the two are one;
We brethren are," he said.

And so, as kinsmen met a night,
We talked between the rooms,
Until the moss had reached our lips,
And covered up our names.

Qualities of Venus

Venus is the diva among the planets and, with her idiosyncratic nature, fits very well into the time of adolescence. She is about the same size as the Earth and is sometimes referred to as Earth's twin or Earth's sister. Let's descend to the surface of Venus for a moment, with the time of adolescence in the back of our minds. First we discover that Venus is enveloped by a thick, rapidly rotating, extremely toxic layer of clouds consisting primarily of sulfuric acid, which makes the surface opaque. The Venus atmosphere consists of 96 percent carbon dioxide.

These clouds hold in the heat, which means that the temperature of Venus is largely independent of the Sun. At a scorching 470°C (878°F), Venus is hot, day or night! These clouds also reflect 70 percent of the sunlight, so the planet can best be seen around dawn and dusk, when she gladly competes with the Sun for our attention. In comparison, the Moon reflects only about 7 percent of the sunlight and converts the rest into heat.

Another special feature of Venus is the shape of the craters created by the meteorite impacts. Due to the volcanic nature of the surface, certain impacts formed flower-like patterns. One could notice beauty on the surface here, so very different from the pockmarked surface of

Mercury. Beauty is very important to the diva among the planets, it seems. Another specialty is that Venus does not have a moon. She has emancipated herself, stands for herself. Venus shows this emancipation or uniqueness also in its rotation. Because unlike all other planets (except Uranus), it rotates in the other direction (i.e., retrograde), and scientists are still unsure why that is. In eight years she also draws an almost perfect pentagram in the sky, which was considered the symbol of Venus in ancient times. Venus also rotates extremely slowly, as if she were saying, "Look here, that's me." Do you feel the strong relation to the age of adolescence here?

The metal that belongs to Venus is copper. Copper is typically found in the vicinity of extinct volcanoes—once-dangerous and toxic places on Earth. A proximity to the planet Venus is already evident here. Copper ores also impress us with the diverse colors on their surface. Depending on which other elements copper connects with, a whole rainbow of colors can arise. It is pleasant to hold copper in your hands and, in days gone by, one had the opportunity to do so when digging out coins to buy the small and beautiful things in life. It is also a good conductor of heat. In her practice, Anne often meets clients (especially young people) whose heads are smoldering like a chimney due to endlessly spinning thoughts; at the same time, they have extremely cold feet. This combination causes inner restlessness and hinders sleeping. The solution is often the application of a fine copper ointment to the feet, which directs the heat forces into the feet and cools the head again so that sleep can enter.

The Roman goddess Venus symbolizes femininity and beauty, and she is one of the figures at the art museum most likely to be seen unclothed (as in the famous statue known as Venus de Milo). Venus is connected to the Greek goddess Aphrodite, who was associated with desire and fertility (as in *aphrodisia*). One version of the story of Venus/Aphrodite's birth says that she arose from the sea near the island of Cyprus, emerging from a giant scallop shell (as depicted in Sandro Botticelli's well-known painting). This image of her birth is interesting in light of the fact that Cyprus has extensive natural deposits of copper (hence the shared root of the two words), as well as the fact that mollusks and other invertebrates have copper-based blood systems (rather than iron-based blood like most vertebrates). In addition, one of the symbols associated with Venus/ Aphrodite is a copper mirror, which accentuated her beauty. In the myths, she had many partners, both among the gods and mortals, and these affairs often created problems for herself and others. Cupid (or Eros) was her frequent companion, and together they created mischief by inspiring desire between others. Venus/Aphrodite was at least partially responsible for the Trojan War after bribing Paris into marrying the most beautiful woman on earth, Helen of Sparta, who was already married. Needless to say, trouble ensued.

At the same time, Venus/Aphrodite was also seen as creating order and harmony. In astrology, Venus is the ruling planet of Libra—the scales. The mythologist and Jungian scholar Safron Rossi states: "In Libra we see Aphrodite as a force where beauty is a form of justice."[37] Where do beauty and justice meet? On the one side, we have nature, which is beautiful on account of its inherent lawfulness and orderliness. On the other, we have a potential arising from human activity. Rossi quotes James Hillman: "The myth says clearly that good government, peace, and right order are ways that Beauty shows itself in the world." Here again, we see that the true, the good, and the beautiful are intimately connected.

We know that issues of gender and sexuality are prominent during the adolescent years, and Aphrodite/Venus has an interesting relationship to these issues. Although the typical association with Venus is feminine beauty and sexuality (in a particularly idealized form), she also has a connection to male sexuality and gender fluidity. Sculptures dating from several centuries BC depict Aphroditos—a feminine Aphrodite figure who also happens to have a phallus. Characteristic representations show this figure either lifting their skirt to reveal their surprising appendage, or a nude striking a seductive feminine pose from behind with the phallus visible when the viewer walks around to the front. Later stories described Hermaphroditos, the dual-sexed child of Hermes and Aphrodite. Hermaphroditus was born a boy and acquired his feminine form by merging with a nymph named Salmacis. After their merging, any man who entered her spring developed an effeminate character. And the union of Aphrodite and Dionysis yielded Priapos—the god of garden fertility, easily recognized in images by his oversized penis. Thus we see Venus/Aphrodite as a central early figure in the realm of gender diversity.

The concept of fertility is also worth looking at here for its connection to Venus/Aphrodite. In spite of her other feminine connections, Venus is not primarily associated with marriage, childbirth, or maternal love, which we might say are the objectives or logical conclusions of fertility. In line with the association between Venus and the future, fertility here represents *future potential*. In the adolescent, for instance, we know that puberty signifies the onset of sexual maturity—the point at which procreation becomes possible— but there is a gap of several years between that point and today's culturally accepted age for marriage or childbirth. In other words, the potential to create life is not immediately followed by that reality. The same can be said for other capacities that are just coming online during the adolescent years. We find here another Venus theme—the need for patience. We can see an image of this if we stroll through a garden. For a wide range of plants that produce fruits, the emerging fruits are green—the color of Venus—and they stay green until they are full-grown. Only then do they develop their vivid colors, which signify their maturity or ripeness. If we pluck the fruits too soon, the flavor is bitter and lacks depth. The adolescent needs patience to develop a healthy sense of inner beauty, to develop the resources to confront the many ways the world is broken, and to find their way to a mature experience of love. They need to wait for the right moment to relish in the sweetness of adulthood.

Mirror, Mirror on the Wall. . .

The first mirrors were made of finely polished black obsidian, a volcanic rock. Such mirrors have been found in Ottoman graves from over seven thousand years ago. It is interesting to note here that being able to see one's own beauty and soul took place by peering into blackness. Later mirrors were made out of flattened and polished copper or bronze, which have been found in women's burial sites in Egypt and Greece. The silver mirrors we are more familiar with today were developed later, and the process of binding a thin layer of tin-mercury to a flat piece of glass was a closely guarded secret in late Renaissance Venice.

The cultural history of the mirror probably begins with the smooth surface of a pond, as in the story of Narcissus from Greek mythology. Narcissus was a beautiful young man who attracted the admiration of many other individuals, but he never returned their affections. When one day he saw his own reflection in a pool of water, he fell hopelessly in love with himself. He could approach the beloved object and it could return his gestures, but he could never attain it. When his tears fell into the water and stirred the surface, the image disappeared. In a monologue, Narcissus lamented about the unattainable love object and finally recognized himself in it ("Iste ego sum": This is me). Eventually he died of his unfulfilled love and turned into a flower.[38]

Fairy tales are a great collection of ancient knowledge, and on the theme of mirrors, Snow White inevitably comes to mind: "Mirror, mirror on the wall, who in this land is the fairest of all?" When the mirror replies: "You, my queen, are fair; it is true. But Snow White is a thousand times fairer than you,"[39] the drama takes its course.

Let us pause for a moment and ask ourselves what this copper fairy tale is actually trying to teach us.[40] In his depth-psychological analysis of fairy tales, Eugen Drewerman was able to point out a problem with Snow White that plays into the time of adolescence.[41] There is a stepmother who has a beautiful stepdaughter. Everything is fine until the day the daughter grows into a woman and becomes more beautiful than the stepmother. This shift in the hierarchy is a direct threat to the stepmother, so she sends Snow White into the forest with a hunter, who is to kill her.

In real life, it is less fatal when a mother sees all her pride in her daughter and defines herself through her. In these cases, the daughter is expected to remain in the role that serves the mother rather than grow into her own story. The same can happen with a father and son: he might want to hand over his business to his son, support him in all matters, and be dissatisfied if the son does not perform well. But if the son has the potential to become better than the father, it is not good either, because that would endanger the father's sense of superiority. In psychology this kind of catch-22 situation is known as a *double bind*.[42]

The double bind is paralyzing. It sends confusing and paradoxical messages that the individual finds impossible to navigate. The signals can be communicated through the content of the spoken words, as well as the tone of voice, gestures, or actions. Examples can be: "Do what you want, but don't disappoint me!" "You can stay out as long as you want, but don't come home late!" or "It has to get better, but I don't want any change!" These kinds of double binds arise in part from parents' own inner conflicts. They want their children to be free and grow in their independence, and they want to protect them from harm and keep them from making the same mistakes the parents did. It might be difficult for parents to accept the road their children choose to travel, but it is a gift to them to follow it with a copper gaze. How nice it would be if we adults would take the copper mirror of our youth with us! As we grow older, we could learn not only to see our own reflection in the mirror—with its forgiving copper glow—but also to see others with the same openness and generosity. This softer gaze would mean more sympathy for all our children's quirks.

In short, the first human mirror was the clear, calm water. When the calm is there, the light is right, and our gaze is at the right angle, we then see our own reflection. But we are also free to change our perspective, and what do we see then? The depth!

Imagine that you have three different mirrors: silver, copper, and obsidian. The silver mirror reflects what is on the surface without distortion. The copper mirror adds warmth and forgiveness to what is given. And the obsidian mirror passes through the surface to reflect the quality of the soul. Which aspects of your own beauty do you see in each one?

In Living Color

See if you can remember walking down the corridors of your high school. Who do you see? Although the names vary depending on where you grew up and when you were in school, many of the groups are easily identifiable: the greasers, the punks, the nerds, the preps, the jocks, the beatniks, the hippies. And the easiest way to distinguish them was by their style—the clothes they wore (and how they wore them), how they did their hair, the kind of makeup they did (or didn't) wear. We not only primarily wear our colors on the outside like the copper ores described earlier, but we also create the looks that tell the world who we are and where we fit. Throughout the realms of plants and animals, color is rarely hidden away—it's usually right on the surface, and prominently placed at that. The colors of flowers serve as an invitation to pollinators, while the colors of animals provide camouflage, signals to potential mates, and warnings to predators. If these color cues were internal rather than external, they would cease to be functional. If a predator could only tell a poisonous frog by its blue spleen, both the frog and the predator would lose. So in the realm of life, color is communication.

Adolescents understand the communicative power of color perfectly well. Whether they are experimenting with makeup or dying their hair pink or wearing the jersey of their favorite sports team, their style is their first word when they enter the room. Even in street gangs, the color of your handkerchief can mean the difference between life and death. With these colors and styles, the youth express to themselves and others where they fit in the social order, or sometimes show that they do not want to fit into the social order. And it's not unusual for adolescents to change characters from time to time to try on new identities—trying to find something that feels authentically like themselves and that is accepted by the desired peer group. In psychology, the idea of *optimal distinctiveness* captures the quest for balance between standing out as individuals and remaining connected to the collective.[43] We may adopt the style of the group we want to be connected to, and then add our own individual touch as a sign of our uniqueness. Or, when we're feeling a little more isolated or alienated, we might track back toward center.

As we move into adulthood, things seem to stabilize somewhat. The group distinctions mostly fade away, and the visual cues mostly point to what kind of career or vocation the person might have. For most, the aesthetic flairs—the makeup, the hair dye, the accessories—become more subdued. They're no longer broadcast signals, but rather ones that might only be detected by those in close proximity: "Are those new earrings?" "Did you do something different with your hair?" In adulthood, we go against the grain of nature and turn our colors inward. We talk about colorful personalities and using colorful language. Our moods even have colorful names—from being green with envy, to seeing red with anger, to being tickled pink with satisfaction or as white as a ghost when we're frightened. As our inner sense of self develops coherence and a color palette of its own, the outer manifestations of color become less necessary to convey who we are.

However, Venus tends not to act out of necessity. Venus would rather be a little spontaneous, a little edgy, a little superfluous. To Venus, the question is not whether I need that new dress, it's whether I look good and feel good when I put it on. And yes, maybe it's even about whether I turn some heads when I walk into the room wearing it. Step back into your youthful consciousness and remember what it's like to spend hours every weekend detailing your hot rod, to find the perfect barrette to complement your outfit, or to add one more sticker to your guitar case or car bumper. In the business of daily life, it's hard to justify taking the time for these extra steps, but Venus doesn't like to take no for an answer—she wants to entice you into little moments of *joie de vivre*.

It's (Not) Black and White

And what about the rainbow of natural hues that people come in? Here we encounter one of the great difficulties of the human world—the issue of color-based racism. In the United States, as in other countries, this beautiful spectrum is reduced to a few color categories—Black, White, Brown, etc.—and there is a long history of discrimination on the basis of these classifications. The association between the color white and goodness or purity, and the corresponding association between darkness and notions of evil, primitiveness, or impurity are ancient. We see them throughout Western folklore, including popular fairy tales. They also exist in the Judeo-Christian religious stream, where light is associated with good and darkness with evil. And, in a sense, they were codified by science in Sir Isaac Newton's treatise *Opticks* in 1704, where he demonstrated convincingly that white light contains all colors, while black represents the absence of color. Three centuries later, we continue to reckon with the very real consequences of an artificial race- and color-based hierarchy. (And while this short section in our book is obviously not going to solve the problems of White supremacy and racism, we hope that by looking at this issue through a different lens it can spark creative thinking for new paths forward.)

Nearly a hundred years after Newton's treatise was published, when its conclusions were well accepted by the scientific community, the German poet-scientist Johann Wolfgang von Goethe decided to challenge it. Why not? Goethe's approach to science was phenomenological rather than theoretical, and he was critical of the tendency for scientists to draw conclusions prematurely.[44] To Goethe, to understand something, one first has to observe it from every angle, gathering observations and fitting them into a general picture.

To Goethe, light and dark—like day and night—are two fundamental aspects of experience, and he was just as interested in the phenomena of darkness as in those of light. In particular, he noted that color only actually appears in the interplay between light and dark. If you were to stand in a pitch-black room, you would not be able to perceive the colors of the objects around you—their colors are not inherent to them, but arise in interaction with the light. Likewise, if you flooded the space with white light of comparable intensity, the colors would be washed out like an overexposed photograph. He observed that when looking through a prism, colorful spectra only appear at the interface between light and dark regions. And, interestingly, you only get a half rainbow at each edge—violet-blue-cyan on one side and red-orange-yellow on the other. In the classic Newtonian approach where you look at a beam of light against a dark background, the color green (and the full classic rainbow) only appears when the band of light is sufficiently narrow for the yellow to mix with cyan. If you reverse the process, putting a dark obstruction in a beam of light, the half-rainbows reverse position, and the color magenta appears at the center of the inverse rainbow that spans from yellow to cyan.

Now, this might seem an odd digression for a section that opened up the issue of race and racism, but there is a fundamental point. Whereas Newton's approach tries to describe how color *is*, Goethe is grounded in the way color is *experienced*. While it may be true in a purely materialistic sense that black is the absence of color, *experientially*, black and darkness have a reality. If you've ever stared up at the night sky while camping in the wild, or seen a sunset that looks like the aftermath of a Holi festival, you know this to be true. Interestingly, in the realm of race and racism, White is considered to be the absence of color. "People of color" refers to non-White people, and historically speaking, only a small amount of non-White ancestry is needed to place someone in that category and open them up to all of the judgments and differential treatment that it entails.

Nowadays, one way of resisting the reality of racism is to say that one is *colorblind*—"I don't see color . . . I treat people based on whether they show me respect, not what they look like." But what does it mean to claim colorblindness? Those who have true colorblindness have to somehow navigate a world that is full of rich meaning and symbolism that they cannot see. A simple statement like, "We're the house with the red door—you can't miss it!" becomes a puzzle to be solved. Colorblindness is not comic-book style x-ray vision that allows one to see through the surface to what lies beneath—someone's "true colors." If color appears at the interface between light and dark, then we will find racial colorblindness away from such edges. To see the full depth of color of the other—to penetrate through the surface to the soul and spirit levels—means to step up to the edge and gradually (and mutually) close the gap between you.

Parker Palmer wrote that love is the only path to true knowledge because to know something we have to enter into relationship with it.[45] Only by allowing ourselves to be known by the thing will it reveal itself to us entirely. In other words, knowledge requires vulnerability and connecting with subjective experience rather than detached objectivity. For White people, it can be painful to see color and to acknowledge the ways that we have benefitted from our own "lack of color." It would be nice to understand the effects of racism and to find a path beyond racism without connecting ourselves to that story personally, but that's not how it works. And it can be painful to be rebuffed when stepping up to that edge, when we make a good faith effort to learn more and understand from those who have born the brunt of this history. When it comes to relationship, however, we don't get to set the terms unilaterally. We find that we need patience in the same measure as our vulnerability to create and hold the space where true encounter can occur.

Maybe you've had the experience of looking outside during a rain shower. On one side of the sky, you see the dark violet-blue clouds that are producing the rain, and on the other side you see yellow-orange sunrays bursting through. "Rainbow weather!" you think, and you drop what you are doing to see. You put on your boots and rain jacket, walk to some open place where you have a good view, and start looking around semi-frantically, hoping not to miss it. If anyone walked or drove past at that moment, they might think you'd lost your mind, but the importance of your quest is beyond what other people think of you. You look and look and might even start to grow impatient—"There has to be a rainbow! But where is it?" Of course, nothing you can do will force it to appear or even speed up the process. Finally, you calm down, start breathing again, and wait. When you see the first hint of color against the sky, everything else disappears. Now you want to stand in the street and stop the cars and point up at the sky. You behold the rainbow as it grows in intensity, as it shifts in brightness across its length, and as it gradually fades away. Perhaps you even notice that the sky is darker above the rainbow and lighter beneath it. You actually can't take your eyes away until it's no longer perceptible. Even though you've seen rainbows before, they never lose their magic. So perhaps this serves as an apt metaphor for interracial encounter: recognizing the potential of an encounter is the first step, followed by stepping up to the edge. Leave your self-consciousness inside, and find patience in spite of your eagerness. Connect yourself fully with the experience, knowing that the rainbow won't always appear, and if it does that it won't last forever. Be filled with the experience, and look forward to the next time that the right conditions arise.

Working with Venus Forces in Daily Life: Dare to Rethink

After all of this information about the youth and their struggles and challenges, the question remains about what the youth can teach us as adults. Now, now . . . we can hear the grumbles coming through the pages. The relationship between the youth and the older generation is notoriously rocky and has been throughout history. Every generation of elders, it seems, has complaints to file about the youth and their laziness or insubordination or coarse language or disconnect from reality. "If children are our future," they quip, "then we're all doomed." And the youth often return the favor, especially when they sense that they are being dismissed without even the effort to understand them. The people of their parents' generation are tyrants and sellouts and hypocrites. How do we break through such an impasse? And what is possible if the youth and their elders can come together to confront the big problems of the world?

As we mentioned earlier, adults can develop a certain kind of amnesia with respect to the passions of their youth. We old folks have all been young in our lives, and hopefully we have experienced the burning fire and enthusiasm of those years. We probably had to struggle with setbacks and disillusionment as we got older, we no doubt became familiar with "how the world works," and at some point maybe we finally gave up on some of our ideals. We can see now how naïve we were to think that we could topple such massive systems as communism, racism, and environmental destruction when so much was pushing back on us, and we had no real resources of our own except our fervent commitment to the cause. Knowing what we know now, we might even feel that we are protecting the youth from disappointment by giving them a "reality check"—"if only they could get it through their heads. . . ."

But what if we turn around the familiar adage and see the youth as our past instead of our future? That is, young people are a living reminder of our own youthful past—our *living past*. If that is true, then partnering with young people could help us to rekindle the fires of our own youth. They can remind us that we have also dreamed of a better world than the one we inherited, and they can make us more keenly aware of the ways in which we are preparing the world that we will hand off to them. They can prompt us to reevaluate what we previously dismissed as unrealistic fantasy—including our own fantasies about who we might become. What would happen if everyone suddenly believed their dreams were possible? If we look into the world, we can see that major structural changes have actually happened in our lifetimes: the Berlin Wall came down; the United States elected its first Black president; and more and more people are trading their "gas guzzlers" for electric vehicles. We may not be able to see our personal stamp on these outcomes, but they happened in part because a vocal minority would not let the issues be ignored any longer.

When we look from the other perspective, we see that the elders are the *living future* of the youth. Just as younger children naturally imitate their parents and caretakers and pretend to be grown up, so do adolescents and young adults look to the world of grownups for role models—people who they can aspire to be like as they age. When they peer into the world and see elders who are complacent, defeated, selfish, and cynical, their youthful frustration can turn into a sense of resignation or inevitability as they move into adulthood. However, when they see strong examples of elders who have never stopped believing in and working toward their ideals, then their own idealism can be buoyed as they meet the hurdles that life will inevitably throw in their way.

When we look at this situation as a whole, we see that the potential of the youth is in their passion, idealism, and sense of urgency. They have a critical eye and dare to offer solutions to our present problems. They have not yet become jaded by bureaucratic hurdles, or at least they are not willing to let such hurdles interfere with their vision. They are still open and therefore can easily get excited about big questions. The potential of the elders lies in their experience and resources, which they have accumulated over years or decades while having been plugged into the "real world." They know how to successfully navigate the bureaucratic machinery to get things done. They've built up social and financial capital that can be invested in ideas they believe in. Perhaps they've even learned that collaboration takes more time, but it can be worth it if it means broader buy-in for the project.

Isn't it time to give ourselves over to this new thought? By working together and taking all age groups seriously, we immediately satisfy the basic needs of human beings: to be heard, to do meaningful things, and to be a valued part of a community. The young ones can develop confidence in the future, and the elders can take on a new leadership role. They can provide the framework and resources for innovation and intervene only when necessary. By dealing with their living past in the young people of today, outdated burdens and structures can be cast off, and they can rejuvenate inwardly as their bodies grow older.

Both sides (and everyone in between) have to dare to take a step toward each other. But just this kind of risk is needed to realize the potential of true intergenerational collaboration, which can make people grow beyond themselves and start working together to address the issues that affect everyone. This kind of collaboration can happen when people can see each other as striving human beings who have gifts to offer that they themselves lack. With that perspective, a genuine encounter becomes possible, out of which can arise what must arise. What this something *is* must be revealed in the encounter, because only there lies the truth to be grasped.

Friday: One Day of Beauty

Here is one last thought experiment on this topic: Let's imagine the world *without* any beauty. This does not mean that everything has to be ugly, but that everything we see around us is reduced to its functionality. The chair is there to sit on, nothing else. The table is set, but nothing more. The clothes fit like a glove and match the weather. Everything works smoothly, but there is nothing superfluous. How does that feel? What exactly are we missing when everything is going well but stays purely functional? What is missing when only the basic needs are covered? It's the beauty. Let's add a timeless design to the chair and a flower to the table and complement the clothes with a beautiful belt. What happens now is something magical. Although the functionality has not been changed, bringing beauty takes the whole situation to a higher level. In this way, space is given to individual creativity, and what was previously nonessential comes to the fore as an act of free expression. By adding even small bits of beauty, one detaches a little from the realities and necessities. We also feel more sublime when the surroundings are beautiful. Venus not only invites us to look for beautiful things, but also begs us to create beauty. For example, we could decide that the day of Venus, Friday, should be declared our beauty day, a day to buy fresh flowers, have a pedicure, pour the chips into a bowl instead of eating them out of the bag, or pay special attention to your choice of clothes. Beauty is never perfection because perfection is exclusive, unplayful, and rigid. Good and true beauty is flexible, changeable, simple, surprising, individual, colorful, inclusive, fun, and has an increasing effect on the functional. Although there are endless ways to express beauty, it is never an arbitrary act—it always comes from an inner source of individual playfulness and inspiration.

"I've found that there is always some beauty left—in nature, sunshine, freedom, in yourself; these can all help you."

—Anne Frank[46]

4

SUN

The Gift of the Golden Nothing

TURN ON THE RADIO RIGHT NOW AND THE CHANCES ARE GOOD you will find a love song playing that you can sing along to. You might be a little embarrassed by the sentimental lyrics, but when nobody else is around you can really belt it out. There is no denying that love songs touch something deep within us. And the allure of love songs is not limited to modern Western popular music. In his book *Love Songs: The Hidden History*, music historian Ted Gioia suggests that love songs have their roots in Sumerian fertility rituals, dating back four thousand years.[47] The genre evolved through the centuries, picking up new themes as ideas of romance, love, and courtship shifted. Even the Bible has a rather salacious love song—the "Song of Songs."

So there is something universal in love songs. And yet, no two seem to be the same. In 2018, a group of researchers published a study that looked at the universality of different kinds of songs.[48] They sourced songs from small-scale societies all over the world that could be classified according to four basic social functions: dance songs, healing songs, love songs, and lullabies. Then they invited listeners from all over the world to listen to brief clips of these songs and indicate which social function they thought the song served. In spite of having no prior knowledge of the cultures or languages, listeners were surprisingly accurate at classifying many of the songs. Dance songs and lullabies seemed to be the clearest, followed by healing songs. However, listeners were no better than chance at classifying love songs. In other words, when they heard a clip of a love song, they were equally likely to think it was a dance song or a lullaby (although love songs were less likely to be misidentified as healing songs).

If we take a closer look at our own love song catalogs, we might begin to understand this finding: Love songs span the gamut of emotional moods. There are songs of yearning, pining for the love that is not yet. There are joyful, playful songs of infatuation, sultry songs of seduction, melancholy songs of heartbreak, and even angry songs of jealously (think Dolly Parton's "Jolene"). We might have them classified into different genres in our music libraries, but in terms of social functions, each in its own way expresses one's love for another, and we experience them that way. They are all love songs.

There is a lesson in here about love: When we choose to love another person, we can't only choose the happy and pleasant sides of love. We have to sign up for the full package. We have to accept the possibility of separation, heartbreak, jealousy, and grief in order to gain access to the joyful and ecstatic sides. If we attempt a "safe" version of love where we shield ourselves from love's challenges, we also cut ourselves off from love's full potential. Love requires a free choice to let go of concerns about what might go wrong and live completely in a liminal space, out of space and time, where that love can grow without bounds.

In other words, unconditional love is an act of freedom—an assertion of our freedom to place ourselves in situations that might bring us pain. In the Buddhist tradition, there is recognition that nothing is permanent—that all sources of joy are only temporary. Or, as Robert Frost put it, "Nothing gold can stay." When we become attached to these sources of joy, we create a source of suffering for ourselves. The answer is not to avoid pleasure or a life full of joy, but rather to live fully in that joy while it is present, and then freely let it go. We can approach these sources of joy with gratitude for what they brought to us—happy memories, life lessons, generative creativity, or new interests.

And if you are like us, whatever twists and turns your love stories might take, you can find a song that resonates with that experience— one that amplifies the joy or commiserates with the sadness or provides a wistful accompaniment to the yearning. Music is a uniquely human tool that we have for capturing, expressing, and sharing our experiences; composers and musicians have a way of channeling the subtle spiritual energies that stand behind human experience. In fact, in traditional Indian culture, musicians are revered as holy people. Finding the right song for your mood makes you feel instantly not alone in your experience. So the next time you're at a party and Neil Diamond's "Sweet Caroline" comes on, feel free to join everyone else in singing out the chorus, knowing that you are all connected in the human experiences of freedom and love.

> Reflect back on a time when you felt totally in love and find a song that was with you during that time. Then reflect on a time when you experienced heartbreak and find a song that was present with you then. Go back and read the lyrics of both songs. Do you find any connections between them? Where do these songs live in you now?

3 – 2 – 1 . . . For Real?

When she celebrated her 21st birthday, the place was packed. Everyone brought cheap beer, she didn't even know all the guests, and that made it all the better. It was loud and wild. The next day they found that the walls were decorated with messages in permanent marker, and the carpet had a burn hole from someone's cigarette. So those who were still there, despite the hangovers, unceremoniously went to the hardware store for brushes and paint and got to work. When she turned 30, she knew all the guests. They brought funny little gifts and good wine. At the big dining table they ate, laughed, and talked, and shortly after midnight the party broke up and everyone went home full and satisfied. When she turned 40, only a handful of friends came. Many others had reasons they couldn't make it, such as lack of a babysitter, crisis in the marriage, work overload, or just being on a vacation. There were vegan appetizers and matcha tea, and charitable donations were made in lieu of gifts. The conversation revolved around healthy eating and body optimization. At 10:00 p.m. they said goodbye. When everyone had left and she dropped into the sofa, memories of the wild birthdays of her younger years returned, and an unpleasant thought crept up in her: *For real? Is this what it means to be grown up? This life of peace and security is nice, but being young was a lot more fun.*

You have an idea for a project, and with a magical enthusiasm you throw yourself into the challenge. You form expectations, you work and stick to your plans, and finally you reach the end. But instead of pure satisfaction, you find a hint of disillusionment. After all the time and effort, it hasn't turned out quite the way you thought it would. Once again, you bump into that unpleasant question: *For real? Is this what I worked so long and hard for? I thought things would be better once I got here.*

These examples paint a rather gloomy picture, and the question is whether this disillusionment must necessarily arise. Let's take a closer look at the period between ages 21 and 42, which Rudolf Steiner links to the Sun. In the first 21 years, we went through various stages. We learned to walk, talk, and think; we went to school; and we tried to master our feelings, relationships, and sense of identity through puberty. The world is open to be conquered by our individual life plan. 3 – 2 – 1 . . . logical!

Now let's take this little countdown as an orientation for this time of life.

3—In numerology, the number 3 stands for, among other things, positivity, communication, and boundless optimism. It is full of youthful strength, joie de vivre, and curiosity. In the ideal case, the person stands exactly there at age 21! They shine brightly, are full of zest for action, and step fearlessly into life. What does the world have to offer me? In the words of Shakespeare: ". . . the world's mine oyster, Which I with sword will open."[49] Between ages 21 and 28, the first of three soul qualities develops, which Rudolf Steiner calls the *sentient soul.*

Here, we see feeling as the basis for action: One feels that something is right and goes for it. When it no longer feels right, there are no qualms about walking away from that job or relationship or apartment. It doesn't matter that the individual still lacks experience in life because this phase is all about gaining experience and learning what they are capable of and what their limits are. Parents sometimes shake their heads in disbelief, for they have secretly hoped that puberty was over now that their child is "all grown up," and now they see a similar spectacle taking place. But this time is different; it is the beginning of the sentient soul phase of stepping out into life with gusto. Back at the birthday party of the 20-year-old, we could hardly hear our own words over the booming music, and all of the fun we had was fun that we had created. We find the qualities of the 3 in this party.

2—The number 2 stands for polarities. *I* and the world are perceived in such a way that you want to connect them. Teamwork, mediation, diplomacy, and intuition are powers of this number. Toward the end of their 20s, a person is at a different point. There is a growing desire for commitment and stability, and individuals now start to wonder in earnest how they can make an impact in the world. The world no longer has to be at one's service, and expectations of perfection are chilled. A job could become a career or a partner a spouse with 80 percent of the ideal—a thought that would have been unthinkable a few years earlier. It becomes clear that thinking takes on a new and stronger importance, and feeling gets a little less weight. Into this time the *intellectual* or *mind soul* unfolds. One can say that it is the center of our soul. One becomes more and more aware of oneself and is ready to tackle even longer-term projects, perhaps starting a family, pursuing a career, or studying a subject deeply. Let's pay a visit to the birthday party of the 30-year-old. Everything is somehow more *adult* like. Instead of the cheapest beer, there is nice wine to be sipped, tasted, and judged. The music plays softly in the background—enough to be noticed, but not enough to interfere with the conversation. The conversation itself touches on topics that reflect a certain amount of life experience and sophistication. These are individuals who have lived a bit and who are fully engaged with life's possibilities.

1—The number 1 stands for unity, leadership, power, and action. The 1 forces us to look at the current situation and gives us the power to change the circumstances. It invites us to take the future into our own hands and to welcome the new. It helps us on the way to independence. But doubt is also part of 1 and there is a hidden fear of making mistakes. In your mid-30s, you may notice that there is suddenly more criticism coming your way. Things that were once easy are now challenging. The tasks that you willingly took on are now becoming burdensome. Unpleasant questions emerge from the depths to the surface: What do I really want? Why do I feel empty, even though I have everything I want? Who am I really? And what do I want to achieve in the world? These questions can also remain unheard for a long time in the chaos of everyday life. The *consciousness soul* begins to awaken. One becomes aware of oneself in a new way. It feels as if the life one has lived is not yet their own. The feeling of emptiness or being alone comes from the fact that every human being is just an individual—an *indivisible* in the truest sense of the word—and this unity or indivisibility is the epitome of the number 1!

If we return to the birthday party of the 40-year-old, we might find that many members on the invitation list are easily stressed. Engagements—even fun ones like friends' birthday parties—have to be planned well in advance in order to happen at all. Before someone can commit, they have to cross-check half a dozen other schedules, from their partner's work to their children's activities, and decide whether they can squeeze in one more thing. Many will send their regrets, along with a classy and practical gift. Even the host will have to find the time to clean the house before the guests arrive to provide an air of "having it together." Since everyone is struggling with this "who am I" question more or less consciously and age is starting to make itself felt, the celebration tends to take place under the seal of health, optimization, and self-discovery. The conversation might focus on catching up and sharing new favorite recipes or fitness routines. At the end of the evening, friends will excuse themselves, say how nice it was to see everyone, and hope to still get to bed at a reasonable hour. For real?

How can we understand this curve of disillusionment arising out of a path that started so joyfully? The Swiss psychiatrist and psychoanalyst Carl Jung put it this way:

> Thoroughly unprepared, we take the step into the afternoon of life. Worse still, we take this step with the false presupposition that our truths and our ideals will serve us as hitherto. But we cannot live the afternoon of life according to the program of life's morning, for what was great in the morning will be little at evening and what in the morning was true, at evening will have become a lie.[50]

Jung compared the course of human life to that of the Sun. The ascent to the height of noon is followed by a gradual descent toward the afternoon and evening of life. In the birthday scenes described earlier, we see the late morning giving way to the early afternoon of life by the early 40s. He speaks of the "biological orientation" in the first half of life, which is about building our sense of identity, importance, and security. This is followed by the second half of life—the "cultural purpose"—that is now in the service of the True Self or soul, your inner and inherent identity.

To achieve the latter goal, however, what has been learned so far is no longer sufficient. For what the youth found externally, as it were, and had to find in the outside world, mature adults must find and give shape to on the inside in the afternoon of their lives. To do so, they must confront some challenging questions: Where do I actually stand in my life right now? Will my life continue on the way it has until now? How does my past relate to my future? This approaching seriousness heralds the arrival of the afternoon of life. The focus of life slowly turns from the outside to the inside. But to take some weight off the heaviness, Marie-Louise von Franz, a Swiss psychologist and longtime colleague of Carl Jung, explains: "The only adventure that is still worthwhile for modern [people] lies in the inner realm of the unconscious psyche."[51] With this in mind we don't need the 40s to be the new 20s anymore, we have a lot we can do! At the same time we are excited to receive the invitation to our 50th birthday!

> **Choose a theme that is currently with you in life. Which stage of this process are you in with this theme? Are you a 3 (optimistic and energized), a 2 (working to balance polarities), or a 1 (leadership, action, and solitude)?**

Keep It Simple

There are certain archetypal characters that appear in many folk and fairy tales across many cultures. One of the most consistent is the *simpleton*—typically a young man considered by others to be of low intelligence and ambition. He is sometimes placed in contrast to his older brothers, who are portrayed as clever and cunning. And while you might think that such a character would end up the butt of a lot of jokes, the opposite tends to be true. That is, he is successful where others fail and often ends up a king. How does he manage this kind of transformation, and what lessons does the simpleton have for us in the twenty-first century? Perhaps a couple of examples will illustrate.

In a Russian tale known as "The Fool of the World and the Flying Ship," there was a family with three boys—two very clever ones, and a simpleton.[52] When the Tzar decreed that the person who brought him a flying ship would marry his daughter, the clever ones eagerly set out. Their mother made sure to send them on their way with fine food and corn brandy. The story, however, says nothing more of their effort. Instead, it follows the simpleton, who begged his mother to let him try, too. Finally relenting to get him out of her hair, she sent him on his way with old crusts of bread and water. He had not gone far when he met an old man who asked where he was going. The boy gladly told the old man, but admitted he didn't know how to make a flying ship. The old man asked if he would share his food, and although he was embarrassed by what he had to offer, the simpleton nevertheless agreed. To his surprise, his crusts had been transformed into fine food and his water into corn brandy. The old man blessed him for his generosity and gave him instructions on how to acquire a flying ship. He also instructed the boy to give a ride to everyone he met on the way to the

Tzar's palace. The simpleton did as he was told, acquired the flying ship, and set off. He met all kinds of interesting characters along the way—from one with an unquenchable thirst to one who tied up one leg to keep from moving too fast—and he gave a ride to each one. But because the Tzar was reluctant to give his daughter to a simple peasant, he set all manner of trials for the simpleton, but each of his trials was overcome with the help of one of his passengers. And so the simpleton did marry the Tzar's daughter, who loved him very much, and he was long revered thereafter for his cleverness.

From Japan, there is a story called "Mr. Lucky Straw" that illustrates another side of the simpleton archetype.[53] The story starts as a man called Shobei falls down the stairs that lead to his village. When he comes to, he finds a piece of straw in his hand. He decides that he must have been meant to have this straw, so he keeps it as he heads on his way. A little later as a dragonfly is buzzing around his head, the simpleton catches it and ties the straw to the dragonfly's tail. A little boy sees him with the dragonfly and begs his mother to let him have it. Shobei freely gives it up, and the mother offers him three oranges in appreciation. Then he passes a peddler on the roadside who is dreadfully thirsty. Shobei gives him the oranges to quench his thirst, and the peddler gives him some beautiful cloth that he had been taking to the market. Shobei thanks him and continues on. Soon a magnificent carriage pulls up alongside him. A princess inside the carriage notices the beautiful cloth and asks him if she could have it. Once again, Shobei freely gives what he has. In return, the princess gives him a bag full of gold coins. He uses this money to buy many fields, which he divides among the people in his village. The village becomes very prosperous, and Shobei is ever after known as Mr. Lucky Straw.

What do these stories have in common? The first and perhaps most obvious is the protagonists' generosity. In both cases, the simpletons freely offer what they have to whoever asks for it. In other simpleton stories, such as the Grimm's story "The Golden Goose," the clever brothers' lack of generosity is made even more explicit: "If I give you my cake and wine, I shall have none for myself; be off with you." Second, the simpletons don't put on airs about their agenda or try to maximize their gains. The Fool of the World told the old man exactly what he was up to and didn't pretend that he knew what he was doing. And when Shobei saw that the princess was interested in his fabric, he might have tried to squeeze her for more riches, but it never crossed his mind. We could say that both of the protagonists operate with complete trust or faith in humanity. And third, even when they reach the pinnacle of their success, they maintain their humility. They never turn their power against others, seek revenge against those who disrespected them, or demand the respect of others. Rather, they earn the respect of others through their actions.

Now, if these characters were regarded as simpletons when these stories were recorded, they might not last ten minutes in today's world. But perhaps the simpleton still holds important lessons for us. First, when we are cynical and overprotective of our own interests, we create a barrier between ourselves and the help that is potentially available to us. We effectively isolate ourselves out of a fear that others will try to take advantage of us, and perhaps we even take pride in our willingness to tough it out on our own. But the simpleton has a different approach. In *The Alchemist* (whose protagonist is a kind of modern-day simpleton), Paulo Coelho asserts, "[W]hen you want something, all the universe conspires in helping you to achieve it."[54] The simpleton has an intuitive sense for the expansive help that is available to anyone open to it. The

Fool of the World trusted that anyone he met after setting out on his journey would guide him in the right direction. Shobei trusted that the straw he found in his hand after his fall must have been given to him for a reason, although that reason was not clear. So when you commit yourself to a certain path, the lesson of the simpletons is to open yourself to the possibility that the people and experiences you meet along the way are there to help you along, even if it's not clear at first what they could possibly offer you.

A second important lesson from the simpletons is to be aware of and overcome any sense of deservingness or entitlement. Sometimes these feelings come along when we are successful at something we set out to do. In that moment, we forget about all of the helpers and good luck that we met along the way. We forget the unexpected opportunity that popped up, the friend who loaned us money to get started, the intern that pulled together needed information, or the spouse who took care of things at home so we could focus on the project. Instead, we feel entitled to the spoils of our success. On the flip side, there may be times when success eludes us, when one effort after another ends in disappointment. Here, too, we may feel like we deserve a good break, as if the universe owes us success after so many setbacks. In both cases, the feeling arises because we see ourselves as separate from the rest of the world, and that somehow the world revolves around us. Just as humanity had to break away from the geocentric model of the universe, in which the Sun and everything else revolved around the Earth, so do the simpletons teach us to experience ourselves as part of the grand movement of life that we cocreate in a grand weaving with the lives of others around us.

It's that simple. "Whoa!" you say, "it's *not* that simple." We are not simpletons. We have a lot at stake. We've been burned before. We have responsibilities and obligations that we need to take care of—a house, a family, a business, a reputation. As Van Halen lead singer David Lee Roth sang, "I found the simple life ain't so simple."[55] How could we even imagine taking up the path of the simpleton in this day and age without completely withdrawing from the modern world? The answer may be to focus first on developing a simpleton way of thinking. In other words, we have to make explicit in our thoughts what is natural and intuitive for the simpleton. If we attend to our initial assessments of many situations, we might be surprised to find mistrust, cynicism, and selfishness. These assessments reflect assumptions that we make about the world. In such situations, we can add a simpleton thought: What if I can be completely honest here? What if I can let go of what I don't need for myself? What if I can trust other people? Having those thoughts doesn't commit us to following through with the action, but it does interrupt the cleverness and self-protection that might represent our initial impulse. It's another way of stepping out of space and time to see the potential to transcend our modern, strategic way of navigating the world. And as we find our courage to start acting on these thoughts, we might find that we are surrounded by more helpers than expected. Of course, we cannot eliminate the possibility of being hurt or taken advantage of, but as we stated earlier, such is the price of love. Yes, the path of the simpleton is a path of love. Imagine what the world would be like if more and more people began to follow these simple steps.

Righteous Anger: An Act of Love

Imagine that you are relaxing in the shade, sipping a coffee at a sidewalk café across from a Buddhist temple in Bali. The birds are chirping, and you are surrounded by the hustle and bustle of merchants who want to sell all kinds of knickknacks to tourists. Suddenly a man in a saffron orange robe arrives, shouts angrily, knocks over the merchants' carts, and shoos them away. "What's wrong with *that guy?*" you wonder. "Who does he think he is to disturb our peace?"

Or imagine that you are sitting at the train station, enjoying the back and forth of the travelers while you wait for your train to arrive. Then suddenly you observe a heated scene. A woman leans over the counter and shouts obscenities at the railroad clerk about the (unavoidable) delay of her train. Through the rage you hear something about an important business meeting that will be missed. She is not calmed down even by her traveling companion, and you notice a worried expression on the clerk's face. "Just because you're having a bad day doesn't mean you have to ruin it for the rest of us!" you think to yourself.

In both of these situations, a typically peaceful scene is interrupted by an outburst of anger. A heated situation boils over, so to speak, and everyone who witnesses the scene feels a little burned afterward. Let's turn down the heat to understand what such situations might have to teach us about Sun qualities.

We can see in the language of emotions that warmth is an important aspect of how we express feelings. A warm greeting is friendly and full of interest, while getting the cold shoulder is decidedly unfriendly and disinterested. Some people feel hot under the collar in high-stakes situations, while others are cool as a cucumber. Love is typically a warm feeling, but as we discussed in the opening section of this chapter it is next-door neighbors with some much hotter states like passion, jealousy, and anger. In everyday language, we use terms like "fiery" or "burning" to describe these emotions. This connection between warmth and emotions is linked to how we feel emotions in our bodies. A research study from a Finnish research team asked a cross-cultural sample of people to indicate which parts of their bodies feel more activated or less activated when they experienced different emotions, and they used these responses to create "heat maps" for each emotion.[56] Emotions like anger, happiness, anxiety, and pride all showed high levels of activation, with the areas around the chest and face being the most consistently activated regions, demonstrating that our faces often show what our hearts are feeling. Anger stood out from the other emotions, however, in that the hands also showed high levels of activation—in other words, anger wants to *do* something to resolve itself.

An interesting aspect of emotions like these is that their warmth remains for some time after the situation that evokes them subsides. Perhaps you've had the experience of watching the Sun set after a day of hiking. As night slips in and the Moon is not yet above the horizon, you can be seized by the depth of the darkness. But then you notice that the rock you are sitting on continues to radiate its warmth. Some of the power of the Sun has remained. In a similar way, when an evening with friends comes to an end and everyone has gone home, you can sit in your living room and feel the warmth of their company linger for a while. Or your first kiss with a beloved seems to stay longer on your lips, and even memories can evoke this feeling of warmth. This warmth, which was created in the light of the encounter, is a parting gift that everyone involved in the situation can take with them. It might even radiate out from you, and you may find yourself inadvertently bringing some warmth to a stranger's day with an act of kindness or a friendly smile. How much harsher would life be if we could not hold on to this warmth for some time after the experience?

However, here again we have to take the challenging along with the good. Angry situations also leave a lasting impression, and usually one that's not so pleasant. Typical of angry feelings, we may feel the urge to *do* something with this warmth, and before we know it, we are inadvertently taking out our frustrations on an unsuspecting pet, child, or cashier. And these targets may, in turn, continue the cycle. It would be nice if we could stop this merry-go-round of misery and create a different impulse from such situations. Perhaps in order to do so, we need to seek a different perspective on anger, which often has a bad rap in polite society.

Anger is included in most lists of "basic emotions," and it is both present and identifiable across a range of cultures.[57] This evidence suggests that anger evolved to serve both communicative and practical purposes—that is, to let others know that you are angry, and to prepare you to confront the anger-inducing situation. Anger typically arises in circumstances where another person interferes with or harms an individual or something important to them, either intentionally or through lack of care. For instance, if you lose your job to downsizing due to a broad economic downturn, you might feel sad and frustrated, but if you learn that the boss's son got to keep his job in spite of having less seniority than you, you can quickly move into the realm of anger. The behavioral impulse of anger is to right the wrong, defend what is threatened, or take back what was lost, as well as to cause harm to the one responsible to diminish the likelihood of a recurrence.[58] For better or worse, over the course of human evolution, those who could wield the power of anger were better equipped to accumulate resources and defend them against threats.

As time went on and people became more "civilized," overt expressions of anger became taboo. Part of the social contract that makes community work is that individuals resolve their differences peacefully and through the proper channels. Resorting to violence or angry threats to get one's way makes social life unpredictable for others. Anger was even removed from warfare, where calm and calculating leaders began to analyze strategy and dictate orders from a safe distance.

That said, it is abundantly clear that in this civilized age those who hold power can and do perpetrate injustices for their own benefit. Nations invade less powerful lands and claim them for their own. Corporations exploit the Earth's resources for their own profit. Individuals are kidnapped and sold into slavery. Religious leaders take advantage of trusting children and adherents. And intimate partners are held hostage through physical and psychological abuse. Learning about injustices like these should trigger that anger center that we all work so hard to keep in check. And anyone experiencing them directly would have a difficult time containing their rage. Clearly, there is still a place for anger to serve the greater good in the modern world. The late US Congressman John Lewis encouraged people to get into "good trouble, necessary trouble"—to take a stand against the powers that seek to exploit or oppress others to their own advantage.[59]

Let's return to the opening examples and explore the differences between them. In the train station, the angry outburst appears to be fueled by frustration at the personal costs of the delay—a missed meeting. And the target of the outburst, the railroad clerk, bears no personal responsibility for the delay. We don't know the broader context of the meeting—perhaps it would have been personally profitable for the individual, or maybe it would have secured a large donation to a cancer research foundation. Either way, the clerk did not deserve the treatment he received, and we can see in this episode the kind of anger that most individuals work to control most of the time. The warmth that remains after this episode likely leaves everyone feeling worse, with no sense of what could be done better or differently in the future.

The scenario at the temple has a different quality to it. As you reflect on what you observed, you may remember a similar situation from the Bible:

> Then Jesus went into the temple of God and drove out all those who bought and sold in the temple, and overturned the tables of the money changers and the seats of those who sold doves. And He said to them, "It is written, 'My house shall be called a house of prayer,' but you have made it a 'den of thieves.' "[60]

In this case, the outburst is grounded in a sense of moral values. You gather that the religious man sees that a holy place is being dishonored by the selling of trinkets. Perhaps he has been there before to talk to them and to try and get them to move away from the temple, quoting religious texts to support his argument, but they remain because it is a profitable place for them to operate. Perhaps he has tried to work with the local authorities to relocate them, but the authorities have disregarded his request. Finally, he can stand it no longer and engages in this act of civil disobedience. There is a mess to clean up, but no lasting harm done, although everyone in the area still feels the warmth radiating from the scene. This time, however, the warmth has a different quality—it can lead to reflection and potentially a change in future behavior.

You might still have the feeling that it wasn't the right thing to do, or that he should have pursued other possibilities before causing such disruption, but it is clear that there is a kind of virtuousness behind the action. And, in fact, as we look back over the history of protests and protest movements, efforts to disrupt the status quo have often been met with accusations of wrong place, wrong time, or wrong approach. The status quo is comfortable, even if it is not right, and sometimes it is only when it is made uncomfortable that the possibility for change emerges.

Before we end the topic of anger, however, it is important to note that the modern world is rife with acts of violence justified by a particular value system, from fundamentalist suicide bombers to abortion clinic attacks. From *their* perspective, in *their* minds the act is perfectly justifiable, even if to many outside observers it was extreme, unprovoked, and immoral. How can we distinguish reasonable, righteous anger from unreasonable acts of terror without assuming that everyone, everywhere, will adopt the same value system? One fundamental difference is that righteous anger never has the intention to harm. Rather, its aim is to bring attention to the higher value that has been threatened or violated in an effort to motivate change.

Rudolf Steiner described righteous anger in response to injustice and other moral violations as a gateway to more mature responses:

No-one [*sic*] does better at acquiring an inner capacity for sound judgment than a person who has started from a state of soul in which they could be moved to righteous anger by anything ignoble, immoral, or crazy. On the other hand . . . [a]nger can degenerate into rage and serve to gratify the worst kind of egoism. This must be so, if human beings are to advance towards freedom. . . . It is because people can change good into evil, that good qualities, when they are developed in the right way, can become a possession of the Ego. So is anger to be understood as the harbinger of that which can raise a person to calm self-possession.[61]

In other words, it is by allowing ourselves to be taken up by the experience of anger (especially in our youth) that we hone our sense of right and wrong and learn to assert our autonomy. Over time, we can gain increasing control over this impulse and channel it into more constructive and less destructive responses. Here we again come back to love, the golden thread of the Sun: Righteous anger is an expression of love, whereby an individual stands firmly in themselves to call out injustice and awaken others to their own higher potential.

Qualities of the Sun

That the Sun is only an average star would probably not occur to us here on Earth. After all, it is large enough to hold 1.3 million Earths, inside temperatures can reach 15 million degrees Celcius, and it will shine for another 4.5 billion years before it turns out the light for good. One can be awestruck by these numbers! The Sun is the central star of our planetary system, providing virtually all of the light and warmth. Life on Earth and the conditions of the other celestial bodies are dependent on the Sun. Everything literally revolves around it! However, the Sun is also found at the edge of the solar system. The solar winds drive out energy-loaded plasma in the form of so-called "interstellar gasses" as part of the interstellar medium into the open space. In this way, a gigantic plasma sphere is formed, the heliosphere, which expands to about four times the distance of the outer planets. The heliosphere demarcates the edge that separates our solar system from the rest of the universe. So the Sun is both center and outer boundary. This is expressed in the symbol of the Sun, which has a dot in the center of an enclosing circle.

Similarly, we can observe how the Sun stands for balance and right relationship. Here on Earth, we have a "perfect" relationship with the

Sun—it provides sufficient light for plants to photosynthesize and for us to see where we are going, and it provides enough warmth to support a vast diversity of plant and animal life. When we look out into the night sky, we can see billions of other stars, many of which are brighter and hotter than our Sun, and yet we experience the night as dark and cold. We do not stand in right relationship with those stars. Even relatively minor changes in Earth's distance from the Sun could render our home planet uninhabitable. Astronomers have used the term "Goldilocks zone" to refer to this narrow band of distances that are not too hot, not too cold, but just right.

Since time immemorial, humans have been fascinated by the power of the Sun. The pyramids in Egypt, Stonehenge in the United Kingdom, the temple of Konârak in India, and the Mayan temple at Chichén Itzá in Mexico are reminders of the deep reverence for the Sun held by ancient peoples from around the world. And it is no wonder: The Sun has an effect deep within us, it moves us, awakens our interest in being active. As a source of light and warmth, it supports activity and vitality, and as a source of love, it carries these forces deep within us.

How do these Sun forces, with their love power, come into us? Where are they to be found? It is probably not surprising that the heart represents the Sun organ, and the development of the heart clearly shows us how these Sun forces are carried in from the *there* (periphery) and into the *here* (center). Let's take a little trip back in time to the third week of our embryonic development for understanding. There, the first blood islands (capillaries) are just forming at the periphery. In this primitive blood vessel system, a hesitant blood flow begins on the outside. This flow reaches a point where it can go no farther in the "head" area of the embryo. *There*, at the centripetal junction of the blood, the cardiac system is formed. *There*, where the movement stops for a moment, the form, the heart as an organ, is created. The heart is formed in the *there*! We look a bit like a little pencil at this time. There is no curvature yet, no head or belly. Now the heart starts its way into the *here*. As the embryo curves in on itself, the heart moves from above into our newly formed center. The heart has moved from the cosmic sphere into the body, having been developed, one might say, first as a crown above the head. Thus the Sun forces come in through the Sun organ into the center of the human being and will connect the thinking with the will via the feeling.

Our language also points us to the metal belonging to the Sun because we all know people with a heart of gold! Let's dig into the cultural history of gold. It is difficult to imagine our ancient ancestors' reaction to encountering gold for the first time, but it's clear that it made a big impression. Cultures around the world associated gold with the divine sphere and processed it artfully for the worship of the gods and for the burial sites of the most important figures, including in many of the Sun temples we previously mentioned. Interestingly, the current scientific understanding is that the gold present on Earth is not native to our planet. Much of the gold accessible to humans is thought to have been delivered by asteroids, carrying with them the remnants of distant star collisions.

Besides the divine side, there is also a devilish side to gold. It was and still is mined under inhumane conditions, and the associated destruction of the environment is enormous. Various gold rushes throughout history drove thousands into poverty and death, and wars were fought for the sake of gold. The divine connection has largely disappeared today. Most gold today is worn in the form of jewelry or tucked away in the vaults of wealthy individuals and nations. In a sense, the unearthed gold is being returned to the earth, but this time with an owner's stamp. If you took all the gold humans possess together and melted it into a cube, it would have a side length of about 20 meters (67 feet). But just as we protect the heart in the center of our body with the ribcage, 99 percent of the Earth's gold is also protected from prospectors in the Earth's core. The amount of gold that lies there reaches approximately 1.6 quadrillion tons. With these figures one can easily see the two extremes of gold; toward one side the materialization, and toward the other side the spiritualization. According to Rudolf Steiner, the duty of gold is to keep the balance between the material and the spiritual. Once again, we can have the sense of center and periphery. Or, to quote an old proverb: "Where there is light, there is also shadow."

So how could working with the power of gold look for today's people? How can we bring some shadow into glaring light and some light into darkness? Let's look at the properties of gold, its density, ductility, and corrosion resistance and transfer these as possible signposts to a golden heart. Gold is a heavy metal: a liter weighs 19.3 kg (a pint weighs 18.06 pounds). Its ductility, or ability to be stretched, is incredible. From 1 gram of gold you can draw a 3 km (1.86 mi) long wire. Incredibly corrosion resistant, it can only be dissolved by *aqua regia*, a mixture of hydrochloric acid and nitric acid.

Where can we find these qualities in ourselves? The human body— which carries us through life, allows us to experience the world with our senses, and enables us to think freely with our brain—is our instrument for acting upon the world. Throughout life, we must constantly decide whether to orient this instrument toward higher or more materialistic aims. This is our responsibility as we create technologies and make decisions on a daily basis. We can find the ductility of gold in our souls. The soul is connected to the physical human being through subjective states like feelings, desires, and aversions. We can choose to be satisfied in our own limited vantage point and realm of experience, or we can allow ourselves to be drawn out by new experiences and different points of view. By allowing ourselves to experience the full spectrum of emotions and exposing ourselves to new ideas and cultures, we can find that the same amount of ourselves can be stretched almost indefinitely. Also, we find in the spirit the "corrosion resistance" or steadfastness. To stand up for one's life and work, against all temptations, is an act of strength of the spirit. There are many accounts of people—from martyred saints to enslaved individuals fleeing on the Underground Railroad—acting courageously, based on the belief that they have a spiritual center that cannot be destroyed by any human act. Only *aqua regia*, a spark from the divine, so to speak, can herald a change of direction in that place.

Working with Sun Forces in Daily Life: The Gift of the Golden Nothing

Think about the last time you did something helpful for someone else. How did it make you feel? Now think about the last time you asked someone to help you with something. How did that experience make you feel? If you had a choice between doing something helpful and getting help from someone else, which would you choose? If you're like many people we've worked with, you're willing to say that it feels good to be helpful, and it's nice to know you have help if you need it. But given the choice, most people would prefer to do something helpful rather than to ask for help themselves. This asymmetry says something important about us as individuals, and it has important implications for our relationships with others.

Decades of psychological research document this discrepancy. Being helpful often puts people in a better mood, and people may sometimes even do something helpful to improve their mood.[62] This fact is one of the key arguments used to challenge theories of altruism—if doing something helpful improves your mood or makes you feel like a better person, then it's difficult to claim truly selfless giving. Across many relationship types, people like to have a balance between giving and receiving; in less close relationships people may formally keep track of inputs and outputs.[63] There may be less recordkeeping in close relationships, where giving, in particular, happens more freely. However, some research suggests that in close relationships, partners tend to be more sensitive to being in a state of *overbenefit* (i.e., receiving more than they've given), and they can react with increased anxiety.[64, 65] People are less keen on asking for help in general. In a survey that Chris collected from a large sample of American adults, respondents were about one and a half times more willing to respond to a request for help than to ask for help themselves in the same situation. What's more is that when people do get help, they often feel more distressed afterward. Although this may sometimes be due to poorly delivered support, other studies suggest that getting help makes people feel worse because it makes them feel bad about themselves—that they are inadequate, dependent, or inferior.[66]

Of course, we can immediately see the problem here: Everyone loves to help out (many people we meet even self-identify as a "helper"), but getting help often makes people feel bad. We either need to collectively rein in our "helper" spirit to limit the suffering we inflict on others, or we need to find the secret to receiving help without feeling worse about ourselves as a result. From our perspective, the latter is more in alignment with the Hummingbird Principle, which invites us all to contribute what we can to face the challenges of the world. If we hold back our help, we withdraw ourselves from our relationship with the world and others and keep to ourselves the gifts we have developed through experience. Perhaps if we turn things around we can begin to see a path forward.

Imagine that your boss announced at the beginning of the year that if your team reached a certain goal, you'd all get a year-end bonus. You are already imagining the family vacation that you'll use the bonus money for. Everyone works hard, and your team reaches the goal. As the end of the year approaches, your boss congratulates your team for their hard work. And then she gives you the option of taking the bonus money for yourself or donating it back to the company to use for upgrades to the employee lounge. Would you take the bonus or give it back to the company? If you find that your boundless generosity has suddenly evaporated and that you take the money for yourself without a second thought, how do you reconcile this choice with the earlier sense of selfless giving in your relationships?

Giving and receiving, it seems, are more than just transactions—they are communication devices that are intimately connected to our sense of self-worth. In our close relationships, helping is one way we demonstrate our worth—we are worthy because we are capable of being helpful and willing to do so. On the other hand, needing to be helped can make people feel like a burden to those around them—even if their loved ones don't see it that way. Public giving such as donating to charities, the "needy," or the "disadvantaged" can provide a little morale boost: "I'm such a good person!" At the same time, people may speak disparagingly about those who benefit from public programs, insinuating that they are "freeloaders." The communication changes at work, however. There, people *earn* what they get, and the value of their contribution is communicated through wages and compensation.

A person would have to be a simpleton to freely give up what they worked so hard for!

How can we leverage the power of the Sun to find balance in giving and receiving? The Sun says to let go of our emotional attachment to giving and receiving, which are only proxies for our worth. The Sun in us is worthy regardless of how much we give or take. And from that place of worthiness, we can deepen our experience of life by allowing ourselves to be vulnerable, to enter deeply into relationships with others, and to create opportunities for personal growth. The Sun bares all to all every day—it keeps no secrets from anyone willing to bless it with interest and attention. In our willingness to see and be seen by others—in our strengths and in our weaknesses—we allow others to shine in their own strengths and to build capacity in their weaknesses.

This last statement points to one of the secrets of giving and receiving: Each of us has certain gifts—some are perhaps with us our whole lives, while others are developed out of experience—that we are able to give freely without depleting our stores. In fact, freely giving these gifts may actually make you stronger or more expansive in your capacities. We call these gifts *golden nothings*. For instance, you may have a keen sense for flavors while cooking and a passion for exploring new gastronomic possibilities. The more you connect with others through the gift of flavor, the more you develop in that capacity. Or maybe you have an intuition for accounting and love to track the flow of money through organizations. You may seek out opportunities that challenge you, helping others while sharpening your own skills at the same time. You know when you are in this place because you experience flow, a surge of energy, and the healthy feeling of challenge. When we are able to give the gift of our golden nothings in this way, we can feel confident that we are living in fidelity to our path through life.

You also know when you are not in this place—you feel overwhelmed, confused, or frustrated. These feelings are a good cue to look outward: "Who do I know that might be able to help me out here?" By tapping into the pool of resources at our disposal, we not only help ourselves through difficult situations, but we also deepen our relationships with others, creating a state of mutual interdependence. In psychology, there is a phenomenon called "basking in reflected glory" (or BIRGing),[67, 68] where, rather than being threatened by someone else's superior ability in some domain (or feeling bad about ourselves), we allow ourselves to feel good about being close to someone who is so competent. In the case of receiving the gift of someone else's golden nothings, we can take this a step further: Not only are we close to someone who is so competent, but they like us enough to share it with us. How great is that?

The ability to receive with grace is important to cultivate for many reasons, as all of us will have moments in life when we need to lean on others. We may experience a sickness or injury that keeps us off our feet for some time. We may have an unexpected financial problem due to unemployment, sudden expenses, or marital separation. Or we may experience the loss of our closest companion and need a shoulder to cry on. When we find ourselves in those situations and experience any reluctance to reach out to others, we need only think of how freely we would help a friend in the same situation, how we would never think less of them for asking for help, and how much closer we would be as a result of this exchange of golden nothings.

The Gift of a Buddha—or—
How to Stop Squandering Compliments

"The color of your blouse suits you very well!" "It's okay. I think the pattern makes me look big."

"This cake you baked tastes wonderful!" "Well, it was just from a mix, so I didn't do much."

"I really like your design!" "It's not as good as Sally's. She's much more talented."

Who hasn't experienced moments like these? We get a compliment and almost reflexively we brush it aside, as if accepting a compliment would be bad or a sign of weakness or arrogance. In doing so, we destroy the social momentum of a situation where someone wanted to give us a little piece of gold. In rejecting the gesture, we also unintentionally reject the one who freely offered it. We all know how painful it can be to be rejected, so why are we so ruthless with pushing compliments away? What would it be like if instead we all accepted the compliments offered to us?

"The color of your blouse suits you very well!" "Oh, thank you, it's my favorite color!"

"This cake you baked tastes wonderful!" "Thank you, I think so, too. And you know what? It's a baking mix where all you have to do is add an egg and water!"

"I really like your design!" "Thank you, I'm glad to hear that, because I'd like to submit it to the contest!"

Don't we immediately feel a warmth and a glow in these dialogues, where a small gesture of gold given away is gratefully accepted? Years ago, Anne was dealing with this very issue and shared it with a partner in a meeting. The partner offered her a Buddha as a gift. A very large

Buddha, perhaps made of concrete, but invisible. From that day on she had a task: She was to accept all compliments, and each time inwardly stick a little patch of gold to the Buddha. Adding the patch of gold was a small reminder of the compliment and a visual representation of the gold that had been freely given to her. (There are actually temples where the faithful can buy pieces of gold leaf to stick to a Buddha statue.) Although it was hard to get started, accepting compliments and adding gold patches gradually became easier and easier. Every now and then she inwardly checks on her Buddha to see where the gold is covering. After ten years, it is a good one-third covered and doing very well. She remains extremely curious as to how it will feel when the last piece of gold is added to the Buddha and she can shine completely from the inside.

> Dear reader, if these lines have touched you and you find yourself in them, consider yourself, from now on, a proud owner of such a massive invisible Buddha. We wish you success with patching gold leaves on your Buddha. And then, may you shine from within.

Sunday: The First Day of the Week

In 1976, the International Organization for Standardization decided that the week should start with Monday; the members filed this regulation under ISO 8601. In 1978, the United Nations went along with Monday being the first day of the week. Interestingly, countries such as the US,

Israel, Arab countries, Japan, and China continued to hold on to Sunday as the first day. One might ask if it makes any difference whether the week starts on Monday or Sunday. Let's take a closer look. Traditionally we have a five-day workweek followed by two days of weekend. Friday evening begins the relaxing end of the workweek, when you might meet some colleagues for a drink. Over the weekend, you might read a book, meet with friends, or go on an excursion with the kids. Whatever you do, the more you enjoy this time, the more suddenly and mercilessly Monday morning arrives as a wet blanket and snatches you from your sleep with the siren sound of the alarm clock.

There is no way out of this bind as long as the measure of relaxation lies in the length of free time. However, if our ability to reset can come from the organic organization of time, then whether the week begins on Monday or Sunday can matter greatly. If one feels on Sunday morning that it is the first day of the week, then one has a whole day to mentally and physically prepare for the week ahead. You can use the peaceful, relaxed Sunday mood to look ahead to the coming week, and this calmness in planning can run like an invisible thread through the week. No more waking up with a confused start on Monday morning. Instead, Monday can start more calmly because it is already the second day of the week, which has already been prepared for. So Sunday is about planning and preparing for the future. However, because the Sun embodies the quality of balance, we must look a little deeper into the realm of the future and ask what needs to be balanced to achieve our concept of future.

What is the future? One way to view the future is as *what has not yet been realized.* In other words, in the past certain processes have gotten under way, we grasp them in the present, and they will continue to unfold as time goes on—we are painting our future with the colors of past experience. But if we look at the future as if it were just the space of the not-yet-realized, something strange begins to be noticeable. The future itself remains silent. It contributes nothing of its own to the conversation; it is simply converting input to output. Or to use the metaphor of light: the future remains strangely lunar, only illuminated by the light of the past. In this sense, the future only appears as an imagination in which we implement our projects and plans. This kind of future is relatively easy to plan for—for any given project or activity, we can ask what the next step is and assess whom or what we are waiting for in order to take it.

But is that all? Isn't that only half of the future? If that's the whole story, we assume we can shape the future like modeling clay with our thinking and our ideas. So when we address the future only as an extension of the now, we obviously don't even consider that the future could have its own quality—that it might have something of its own to say. The future is then like an empty box—with the emphasis on *empty*. Because the future will remain a box even if we cram it full. It remains just a container. This is a future without a future.

So, what is the other half of the future? Everyone can recall projects and goals they had that were derailed or lost altogether when something unexpected happened. In the moment, this was likely a huge frustration, but perhaps years later we could experience gratitude for the change of course. Let us imagine that everything we wished for in our youth had actually come to fruition. Aren't there a few things that would be disastrous today? Isn't it wonderful that now and then *something* has entered our lives, that something, or perhaps, *someone* has thwarted our plans and given it a new turn? Aren't the things that come into our lives unexpectedly essential to becoming who we are? It is actually a blessing that our life is not just about what we plan to do—that not everything we wish for will come true. And yet we must be careful not to say—even with a comforting tone—to anyone who is shipwrecked that it is the best that could have happened. No, that would be a false consolation. The shipwrecks of life have to be suffered and experienced existentially in order for their lessons to be revealed to the individual. There is no shortcut wrapped in cotton wool. On the other hand, we wouldn't simply sweep a very happy surprise off the table with a nod. Happiness and suffering and all that lie between are of value and need to be experienced.

The philosopher Stefan Brotbeck discusses these two aspects of the future in his book *Zukunft* (English: *Future*).[69] The stream that flows from the past into the future is called the *Futurum*, and the stream that originates in the future is called the *Adventus*. The Futurum is more about the individual planning with thoughts, feelings, and experiences from the past; it is about becoming. Adventus has a more social quality, something or someone arrives, crosses our path in an unexpected way; it is about arriving.

Some people are more linked to the planning part of the future and other people have a more "wait and see" relation to it. We have to be careful that we do not say that the *Futurling* is simply exaggerated initiative and that the *Adventling* is exaggerated serenity. Both simply have too much of a good thing. Just as we can't choose to only breathe in or only breathe out, we can't expect a future that is entirely within our control. Neither can we entirely turn the future over to fate. The future is made of both of these qualities, and we need to find our individual relationship to them. They are related like two ends of a scale.

But there is third quality that can bring these two into balance: Back to square one! As the first day of the week, Sunday is the balance of the two streams. Practically spoken, you can sit down and plan the upcoming week based on last week's progress, unfinished to-do list items, and events already scheduled: Futurum. Then you can close your eyes and sense into the upcoming week. What can you feel or hear coming toward you? Is there a word, a color, a feeling that you can glimpse?: Adventus. Playing with both Futurum and Adventus strengthens our capacity to be openhearted in the social field. So yes, it makes a difference if Sunday or Monday is the first day of the week. And planning in a Sunday way, inviting both Futurum and Adventus, is possible at any time, no matter what day.

Try it yourself: Next Sunday, sit down and plan the week ahead in the spirit of Futurum. Then close your eyes and try to listen to what wants to come in. Perhaps a question or two will arise, one or more colors, or individual moods or words. Write down whatever they are. Observe in the coming week if they are somehow connected. With this you invite the future in the sense of Adventus.

5

MARS

I Want to Break Free

WHAT DOES IT TAKE FOR A BLACKSMITH TO FORGE A SWORD FROM a bar of steel? A forged blade expresses the merging of two forms of power. First, there is the physical power of the smith. Forging is an intensely physical activity. The hammer itself weighs several pounds, and to raise it and strike the metal repeatedly for even a few minutes would exhaust the inexperienced. But the smith is able to channel an inner power that sustains this activity through the day's work. That said, even the strongest and most determined blacksmith would be helpless without the addition of a second form of power—the power of fire. The fire of the forge has a transformative power on the metal that softens it and makes it amenable to the will of the smith. In other words, the fire—the outer power—and the will of the smith—the inner power—need each other in equal measure. The bar will not become a sword of its own accord.

Moreover, only when these forms of power unite and realize that they both draw from the same well of universal power is the transformation possible. Then, the smith can sense when the metal is just hot enough to work the next step and just how far he can go before he must put it back into the fire. He can feel where to strike and how hard to strike, and he can feel by the recoil of the hammer if he's properly hit his mark. It's a process that can't be rushed—the steel must slowly be drawn out and shaped to preserve, even to increase, its strength. Iron and steel have a grain like wood that the smith must work with. If he heated it to the point of melting (as when making a casting), it would lose the strength of the grain. A cast sword would shatter with the first blow. So when the power of the fire unites with the power of the smith's will, the final object gains maximum strength.

When we think of swords and blacksmiths, our minds are transported back to the days of knights and chivalry. The knight is the epitome of courage—seeking out quests and adventures to defend and protect those in need of such services. The sword is of course an essential part of the knight's kit, but a knight who walks into battle with only this sword would be seen as reckless. By the honor code of the knight, he might not even be able to find an opponent willing to take him on. The knight must also have his armor and his shield—he must be prepared to fend off and even receive blows from his opponent to the same extent that he is prepared to deliver them. The courage of the knight comes from standing firm and fighting for a higher purpose in full awareness of the danger involved. In Wolfram von Eschenbach's telling of *Parzival*, the young hero disgraces himself in his first battle by killing his opponent with a javelin—a weapon not fit for knightly combat because it keeps the attacker outside the reach of his opponent.[70] As with the blacksmith, proximity to the outer fire is an essential counterpart to the fire within. Likewise, when the knight becomes consumed by the inner desire for victory or conquest, he can become blinded to the danger of the situation and suffer an unnecessary defeat. He must control the fire, lest the fire control him. The worthiest battle and the greatest opportunity for achieving honor therefore come when the power within is matched by and unites with the power approaching from without.

Where is the lesson in these stories for the modern person? There is an expression that says we forge our own destiny. In other words, our destiny is not a given—achieving our full potential is not like planting an acorn in the ground and waiting for the oak tree to appear. Instead, it is like the bar of steel—capable of becoming anything that we commit our sustained will to. Shaping it is our life's work, and we must constantly move back and forth between the activity of the anvil and the preparation of the fire. Perhaps you've had the experience of looking at a very successful person and thinking how lucky they are to have everything they want, and then you later read their biography and find that their success required many years of intense effort, adversity, and setbacks. Having good luck can be hard work! So as we step into the realm of Mars, we can begin to cultivate a magnetic attraction between the challenges of our lives and our own inner fire and find the courage to confront these challenges head-on.

Think of something that you've often thought about doing but something has always held you back. Make a commitment to yourself to do it!

Veni, Vidi, Vici

Veni, vidi, vici! I came, I saw, I conquered! That actually says everything about Mars. We could stop here. Determine what is yours, and take hold of it with sword and shield. What a force! But one of the challenges of the Mars phase of life is to step into that power in a healthy and productive way. How we get there is one of the most important journeys of our adult lives.

Perhaps there were already questions simmering under the surface toward the end of your 30s, but now in your 40s there can no longer be any doubt that something has to give. It can feel like waking up from a dream when one day you rub your eyes in disbelief and ask yourself: "Is this what I have been working so hard for all these years? Is this all life has to offer me?" In the early part of this Mars phase especially, these feelings of agitation and disorientation can even intrude upon moments of joy: "I have everything I thought I wanted—a happy marriage, sweet children, the esteem of my colleagues, a nice house, a practical car. Isn't that enough? Why do I feel like something essential is missing?"

You take your shield and sword and make ready to go into battle. But which one, and to what end? In a classic "midlife crisis," the individual immediately looks to the outer world as the source of the problem. "I would be happy if only I had . . . " a younger and more attractive partner, a different job, a car that was more fun to drive. In only a few careless strokes of the sword, one's whole life can be riddled with holes. In other cases, the individual takes a more cosmetic approach—a little hair dye, a little liposuction, some clothes borrowed from the teenager's closet. With either approach, however, it soon becomes clear that these changes are not the solution, and the sense of incompleteness and dissatisfaction lingers on.

Why does this restlessness and zest for action appear precisely at this point in our biography—especially when some have only just arrived in the life they thought they've always wanted? For many individuals, the 30s are spent in a building up phase, with an orientation toward an ideal future. That might mean keeping one's nose to the grindstone at work in an effort to climb the corporate ladder. Or it might mean buying a house and creating a home, or getting married and raising children. In each of these scenarios, there is a major up-front investment of time and effort, justified in one's mind by the belief that down the road one will be happy, financially secure, living in comfort, and surrounded by love. As you step into a new decade of your life, you may start to wonder why you're not there yet. You've put in the effort, you've checked the boxes—what's the holdup? This feeling can be exacerbated when you notice that some parts of yourself are not as they once were. You no longer have the beach bod, and no amount of dieting or exercise can seem to bring it back. Wrinkles have started to appear on your face, which is bad enough, until you notice they have imprinted more worry and frustration than smiles on your visage. Your energy level and libido are waning. And you find that you suddenly need a fully outstretched arm to read the menu at your favorite restaurant, and you need to invest in your first pair of "readers." In other words, for the first time you feel yourself "getting old," but you expected your life to be amazing well before you got old. You feel cheated and lied to, as if all of the things you've been doing in service of your ideal future are not going to lead you there after all. You want to slap the people who say, "Forty is the new twenty!" And you begin to resent all of the ways you've been neglecting (even forgetting about) yourself all these years.

How can we channel this Martian agitation in a more constructive direction? The first step is to shift our focus from the outer world into ourselves. Rather than point the finger at all of the reasons for your frustration, start by acknowledging the strength of your own individuality that wants to assert itself—acknowledge the powerful being that you are. In acknowledging the strength of your being, accept also the responsibility of having made many decisions that have brought you to where you are. You were not simply a piece of driftwood being cast about by the surf, but an active participant in charting your own course through life. In accepting that responsibility, you can seek the lessons that your path has taught you about yourself and the world around you. Has it sharpened you? Brought you clarity? Developed new and unexpected capacities? And yes, perhaps you really have been tolerating a toxic work environment or a partner with whom you are fundamentally incompatible. But from this strength of self, you may see the lessons in those experiences as well and be able to let them go with a sense of gratitude for insights about yourself that may not have been gained any other way.

The psychologist and biography researcher Bernard Lievegoed described what is at stake in this phase:

> In the path of life we now find ourselves faced by a crossroads;
> the choice we make determines the future course of our lives
> and whether a new leitmotiv will be realizable or whether it
> will disappear into the depths of the subconscious, from where,
> for the rest of our lives, it will present a constant threat to our
> feeling of self-respect.[71]

So this is our battleground, and the battle is to reclaim your leitmotiv! But wait—what *is* a leitmotiv? This term, borrowed from German, translates as *guiding motive*. It is the big idea that one's life is ultimately all about, and it lies at the heart of biography work. Clues to the leitmotiv can be found by looking inwardly as well as outwardly. On the one hand, you might ask what drives you, what you're passionate about, what values you hold dear, why you do what you do, what draws you in and what repulses you? On the other hand, you might look at the patterns of experiences that keep coming your way, sometimes despite your best efforts to avoid them. The question of the leitmotiv is ultimately the question of what story you are living out and whether you are willing to take the reins. The potential blessing of this phase is the discovery that you actually have all it takes, all the strength and the stamina necessary to take a firm grip on your life and reclaim your story.

The challenge of this phase is having the courage to do so when your true values, goals, and beliefs diverge from those around you and from how you might have been living up to that point. It always takes courage to be different, and this perhaps stems from overestimating just how similar others are. The personality and motivation researcher Steven Reiss spent years examining why people behave the way they do and what makes them happy. In contrast to other approaches that try to identify a narrow set of basic human motives that everyone is affected by, Reiss found something much more idiosyncratic. His work found evidence for sixteen basic motives that influence how people behave, and that everyone has a more or less unique combination of these sixteen that guide their path through life. These desires include power, independence, curiosity, acceptance, order, saving, honor, idealism, social contact, family, status, vengeance, romance, eating, physical exercise, and tranquility.[72]

If we find, for instance, that we don't seem to value family time as much as our parents, siblings, friends, or romantic partners do, it doesn't necessarily mean that there is something wrong with us. Rather, it may point to something fundamental about who we are and who or what we are capable of becoming. If we can see these idiosyncrasies in this way, then perhaps we can develop interest in them and invest in working with them rather than resisting them. Reiss suggests that these findings could influence our whole approach to education, recognizing that children are not all motivated by curiosity, competence, or a desire to make others proud. Instead of trying to contort the child into existing systems, Reiss suggests that parents and educators respect the child's unique style and meet them where they are. When we recognize that our ways of seeing and evaluating the world are rooted in our own guiding motive, we can better appreciate and accept that others are striving to act in accordance with theirs as well.

And by the time we enter our 40s, we have gained a lot of experience where this leitmotiv was suppressed, misunderstood, rejected, or undetected. But now it pushes itself to the surface to be seen and acknowledged, precisely along the fault lines of resistance that it has experienced. These undermining experiences begin to crack the shell of the person we think we're supposed to be and provide the basis for something new and more authentic to emerge. New questions will arise in this battle of reconquering: Do I have to work as many extra hours as my coworkers, or can I reclaim some time for a side business I've been dreaming about? Do I actually enjoy going out to bars with my friends, or do I prefer to be at home reading books? Do I like going to high-intensity workouts at the gym, or would I rather be enjoying the beauty of nature as part of a hiking or cycling club? There are no parents, educators, or teachers in the way anymore; we stand alone for ourselves, no excuses or scapegoats needed. The battle of reconquering can begin as soon as we identify the cause. Veni, vidi, vici. If we succeed in this fight, we have set the course for our own, individual further life. It's worth a fight.

But wait! One could argue that conquest has never brought peace, and that war has never been based on deep truths. Especially when the "Veni, vidi, vici"—which Caesar confidently and laconically used in a letter to his friend Gaius after the Battle of Zela—testifies to an arrogance and callousness toward an attack that left many dead. Do we really want to participate in this ruthless and unforgiving force? Is Mars, the god of war, asking us to become merciless?

No! We can't leave it like that. The veni, vidi, vici to reconquer our own leitmotiv is neither ruthless nor merciless—it delivers the wonderful potency of transformation. The transformational power takes the shield and sword out of our hands, melts them, and forms plowshares instead. With these plowshares we can now cultivate the fields of our future life. The necessity to go to war has turned into a striving for peace in life—personal and social. With the recognition of our own guiding motive, we can turn our attention and interest to those of others, and this interest becomes the first stone in the pillar of a peaceful coexistence.

Westarctica or Bust!

In August 2001, Travis McHenry, a 21-year-old in the United States Navy, discovered that a vast expanse of Antarctica was unclaimed by any country. Two months later, he sent a letter to the United States Office of Oceans and Polar Affairs to formally claim the land for himself. He named this micronation the Achaean Territory of Antarctica (now known as Westarctica) and appointed himself Consul-General. Veni, vidi, vici.

This kind of imperial ambition has a distinctively Mars quality. We see it, for instance, when a group of children make a "fort" inside their neighbor's hedgerow, complete with a sign that says "KEEP OUT." We see it when a husband claims the basement as his man cave, taking with him the old couch, a kegerator, and an 80-inch television. Or, on the other side, when his wife evicts the lawn tractor from an outbuilding, puts up curtains, and declares it her new she-shed. In each case, the need for a private space comes together with the discovery of a potential location and *boom*!—the claim is staked . . . even if the new spot wasn't exactly "up for grabs."

But this section is not about property seizure. Rather, it's about the social aspects of the Mars gesture. For Mars, it's not enough to simply do something—Mars wants his victory to be acknowledged. In the case of Westarctica, McHenry needed to do more than simply tell himself that that big slice of Antarctica was his. He had to make a public claim—to seek outside acknowledgment that it was his. Now, if you've never heard of Westarctica, it's because this claim has not been formally recognized by any governments, but it has been acknowledged by individuals. Westarctica's website currently claims a population of more than two thousand. It has a cabinet, an extensive peerage system, and a Royal Guard. And members of the Westarctican delegation can mingle and strategize with other micronationalists at the semi-annual MicroCon summit. The reality of the individual achievement is cemented through the social sphere.

The same could be said for the more mundane examples listed above. If a child discovers the perfect spot for a secret hideout, he can't wait to show his friends (and work out the list of who is allowed in and who is not). The husband is eager to have his buddies over to watch the game. And after a thorough cleaning and a fresh coat of paint, the wife can invite friends over to her cottage for a private whisky tasting. These are exclusive spaces, not solitary spaces, and the welcoming of guests creates an opportunity for the victory to be properly recognized with oohs and aahs and covetous expressions.

In life, we are constantly negotiating between the private and the social. We want to be independent and autonomous, and at the same time we want to be accepted and valued. We want time to ourselves, and when we get it we find ourselves wondering what everyone else is doing without us. However, the way we handle this negotiation might look different under different circumstances. For instance, in the Venus chapter we explained the importance of "fitting in" for the adolescent. Standing out is nice, but not at the expense of isolation or ostracism. Everyday actions—from the clothes put on in the morning to whether to raise one's hand in class—may first be subjected to a social acceptability litmus test. It looks a bit different under the influence of Mars. Mars says, "Go big or go home!". . . and wants to make sure someone is around to see the outcome. Mars doesn't even mind an audience when a big risk fails. The high roller who goes "all-in" at the poker table will win the crowd even if he loses the hand.

There is a second way that Mars helps negotiate between the personal and the social, and this might be particularly beneficial for individuals who see themselves as helpers or givers. We are all familiar with the portion of the airplane safety demonstration where the flight attendants describe what to do in case of a drop in cabin pressure. Oxygen masks will drop down, and you should put on your own before trying to help others. In other words, you won't be any good to your neighbor if you can't breathe yourself. Some individuals find it very difficult to prioritize their own needs when they see others struggling. It feels selfish or heartless. Even something less dramatic—such as wondering how you could face your child if you skip their class play to attend an important business meeting—can be painfully difficult. But Mars says that every time you neglect your own needs, you lose a little bit of the air inside your lungs. The effects accumulate over time, and eventually as you run panting from one person in need to the next, you may find that the empty space inside is filling with resentment instead. You feel burnt out, and it's difficult for you to see that no one but you is to blame. So Mars says, please, be a little bit selfish sometimes. Eat well. Exercise. Socialize. Have fun. Keep life exciting for yourself. And when you turn your attention back to those around you, you might find that your willingness to grab life by the horns and put yourself first has motivated them to do the same.

Free Advice

"I want to break free!" Who hasn't had a moment in life where they felt stuck, backed into a corner, or unwilling to tolerate the demands of others any longer? But what does it mean to break free? Who or what are we breaking free from? What would life be like if we achieved the kind of freedom we wish for? And is it even possible? Given that freedom is one of the most hotly debated subjects in human history, it is worth taking some time to examine this idea.

The word freedom may immediately evoke images of waving flags and patriotic songs. The history of the United States is built on a narrative of breaking free from oppression—from the arrival of the *Mayflower* to the Declaration of Independence, and from the 19th Amendment that guarantees women the right to vote to the Civil Rights Act. The movement has always been toward expanding freedoms to groups that were previously oppressed or disadvantaged. However, to focus on the existence of these freedoms without the struggles that preceded them misses one of the most important aspects of freedom—it is never given; it must be fought for and taken. This is true in part because on the other side of any movement for freedom is a countermovement that believes that a change to the status quo is an impingement on *their* freedom. Whether through war, risky escapes, or tense public demonstrations, the fight for freedom is never easy. Freedom, as they say, isn't free.

We could draw parallels to movements for freedom with examples from individual lives: the woman who is held captive by an abusive partner; the undocumented worker who is forced to tolerate inhumane working conditions; the religious minority who is regularly subjected to death threats. To be sure, these outer conditions are unjust and are worthy of an effort to overturn them. In any debate about freedom, however, it is useful to distinguish between outer freedom and inner freedom. Here the question becomes, can such individuals—or any individuals for that matter—maintain a measure of inner freedom despite these outer restrictions?

The psychologist and holocaust survivor Viktor Frankl[73] had much to say on this topic. He drew extensively on his experiences and observations in concentration camps. It's difficult to think of a more extreme example of outer restrictions to freedom. The prisoners were stripped of all possessions, separated from family members, identified by a number rather than a name, monitored constantly, worked to the bone, starved, and beaten with impunity. By all outward indicators, the situation was hopeless. However, he reported surprising moments of vitality and human spirit among his comrades—telling jokes, talking about favorite meals, and going out in the cold to watch a beautiful sunset. Where do these impulses come from? To Frankl, they came from an inner space that is the source of love and meaning and for which the individual is eternally sovereign. No outer conditions, said Frankl, could penetrate that space so long as the individual maintained the will to preserve it. He could choose to share a joke when feeling downhearted, or notice the flowers on the march to the worksite. "[E]verything can be taken from a man but one thing: the last of the human freedoms—to choose one's attitude in any given set of circumstances, to choose one's own way."[74]

So as we come back to the impulse to break free, we have to ask whether the barrier to freedom is internal or external. You may feel trapped in a dead-end job, stuck in a marriage that no longer makes you happy, or blocked from pursuing a lifelong dream. It's not up to us to say whether you need to break free from these outer conditions or how, but we can invite you to ask whether you are truly claiming your inner source of freedom. What different choices could you make that would bring more fulfillment to your workdays? Have you expressed your concerns clearly to your partner and asked for what you need? Have you considered creative ways to take the first steps toward your lifelong dream without disrupting your existing commitments? The sword will never take shape if the blacksmith is afraid to get close to the fire. The knight will never experience the satisfaction of victory (or the accolades that come along with it) if he shies away from the battle. Mars demands that you take responsibility for your own needs and break free from the fears or worries that might be holding you back.

Qualities of Mars

Mars has long held a place in the popular imagination. Our planetary neighbor to the outside, it is a dusty, rocky planet, about half the size of the Earth. Often referred to as "the red planet" because of its reddish appearance in the sky, it has been the imagined home of alien life as well as a potential "planet B" for humanity.

The exploration of the planet Mars began with the invention of the telescope around 1610. During the first three centuries of telescopic observations, the image of an Earth-like and life-friendly planet solidified more and more, so that toward the end of the nineteenth century, it was taken for granted that the red planet was full of life. Dark areas were mistaken for bodies of water and the changes that could be observed through the seasons of the planet were attributed to vegetation. But when, in 1965, the first close-up photographs of the surface of Mars were transmitted to Earth by the U.S. spacecraft Mariner 4, the disappointment was huge: Instead of a planet teeming with life, the images revealed a barren surface pocked with craters—neither of which could provide the atmosphere amenable to life as we know it. The longing for Mars as an alternative planet remains unbroken. Mars missions are being prepared, and somehow the dream of a Martian settlement persists. A flight in a spaceship to Mars would take about six to seven months, one-way. And a radio message from Earth to Mars would take eleven minutes, which of course would make it difficult to maintain contact with the astronauts during a mission. Strong nerves, a clear focus, willpower, and the desire to complete a critical endeavor under all circumstances would be the basic requirements of such astronauts.

The reddish color of Mars comes from the iron oxide that covers the surface as dust. Iron is also the metal that has been associated with Mars. The Earth's core is believed to be primarily molten iron, which has its origins in primeval supernovas—exploding stars whose iron contents recombined into planets like Earth. Much of the iron closer to the surface is the result of meteor showers. So even in the creation and distribution of iron, we can see something of the Mars gesture. Iron extraction began around four thousand years ago and quickly became a material foundation of human culture and civilization. Iron was used in the making of weapons, tools, and agricultural implements well before the beginning of the period known as the "Iron Age" (from 800 BC), particularly in the Hittite Empire (modern-day Turkey).

Mars was the god of war in Roman mythology and the embodiment of masculine energy. While his Greek equivalent, Ares, was often depicted as barbaric and bloodthirsty, the Romans saw Mars in a much more positive light. This is perhaps because Mars was the father of Romulus, the legendary founder of Rome. In the Greek tradition, Ares's sister Athena was seen as a patron of strategy and leadership, while Ares was connected to brutality and control by force. Ares did not have a positive connotation for the Greeks, was rarely worshiped as a god, and even found himself the subject of abuse and humiliation. For instance, when Hephaestus caught Ares in a tryst with Aphrodite, he captured them in a magic net and paraded them before the other gods. In addition, some Greeks observed a ritual of binding a statue of Ares in chains, putting him on trial for murder, and exonerating him as a way of securing his protection against invading pirates.

In contrast to Ares, Mars was more controlled and seen as a means of securing and maintaining peace. He was fearless and he fostered courage among the Roman soldiers. He was also connected to agriculture and springtime, perhaps predating the Latinization of the Greek myths. In the spring (March being the month of the spring equinox), we see the outward gesture of bursting forth, which fits with Mars's masculine connection. Revered as Mars was among the Romans, even the less-than-flattering stories of Ares that became connected to Mars were retouched. Mars's love affair with Venus (the equivalent of the Greek Aphrodite) was typically portrayed romantically, with Cupid or his companion, Amores, working in the background. Their love was seen as true and even came to symbolize the relationship between husbands and wives—a connection that remains in the popular imagination to this day.

Superman and Wonder Woman

If every person really is an individual, then every person also has unique abilities that they can offer the world. The challenge here is to find your own superpowers, those that are uniquely yours and perfectly suited to meet the time in which you live.

A little boy in Anne's practice once asked her if she had a superpower. "Yes, I am Wonder Woman," she responded. He asked: "Why Wonder Woman?" She replied: "Because I always wonder!" What may seem like a small, inconsequential conversation sheds light on something much bigger than it might seem on the surface. This ability to wonder is a force that is essential in her work, and it is a power that deeply belongs to her. This seemingly insignificant question from the boy opened her eyes to the appreciation of a skill that she had never thought much about. Let's face it, how many of us are aware of our superpowers? Or do they disappear into insignificance because we take them for granted? If so, our superhero cape may be collecting dust in the back of the closet, just waiting to be pulled out.

Jason Nazar, a successful American entrepreneur and comic book lover, organizes the core values of his companies around the idea that everyone who works there is a superhero. He has outlined ten lessons that business leaders (or anyone, for that matter) can learn from superheroes.[75] We share them here to support the exploration of your own hidden superpowers.

- **Lesson 1: Superheroes never give up.** A superhero never gives up. The fight is always fought to the end. Tenacity and perseverance are the key characteristics. Superheroes face challenges with an irrepressible belief in success. Perhaps one or the other has shown this perseverance in an apprenticeship, on a hike, or in a difficult argument where it was not clear for a long time whether one could really express one's position. This power can be found in small and large deeds. Where can you find this power in yourself?

- **Lesson 2: Superheroes always get the job done.** Superheroes don't *nearly* save people from the burning building or *almost* bring a driverless train to a halt. They act or they don't act. So you have no excuse not to finish something you have started. Starting a lot and finishing nothing can be crippling to one's process and forward progress through life. Who wants to live on a construction site? Where are all the projects you have started and never completed? Are they serving you?

- **Lesson 3: Superheroes are experts in their field.** Superheroes have very idiosyncratic skills, and they know exactly how to use them. Do you know what you're good at? And are you using these abilities where they're needed? It can be unbearable to work in a team where people are doing work for which they have no real talent. The cook without a keen sense of taste may be much happier when he finally admits that he could use his sense of speed and safety much better as a quality control inspector. It is vital to figure out what one is good at and try to use these qualities where they can best be used.

- **Lesson 4: Superheroes are crystal clear about their purpose.** Nazar uses the example of Captain Marvel here: Even though he is only a 10-year-old boy, he is clear about his mission. "I defend the good!" What is your goal in life? What's your leitmotiv? These are necessary questions, and although we are all happy to avoid them once in a while, they remain stubbornly on our heels.

- **Lesson 5: Superheroes are not flawless.** Maybe that's a bit of a surprise. But sometimes even superheroes need several attempts to achieve their goal. So perfection is not the ultimate goal, but rather striving for perfection. One can imagine that perfection is a lighthouse, which shows the navigator where to sail, though it is not the destination in itself. Striving for perfection allows mistakes and a change of direction if necessary.

- **Lesson 6: Superheroes do not seek glory.** No matter what superheroes do, they don't do it for fame or glory. They are precisely *not* looking for the public's attention. They do their job because they believe in what they are doing. What is it like to be surrounded by people who demand the applause of others after every little effort? These days, many individuals have turned to creating an online presence on social media where they can strive for instant fame. However, they may find that this yearning for recognition actually weakens their ego instead of strengthening it, particularly if the response from the community doesn't meet their lofty expectations. How does it feel to fight for a cause without the laurel wreath in mind?

- **Lesson 7: Superheroes help others.** No superhero needs his strength exclusively for his own well-being. His deeds are always in the service of others. "No man is an island, entire of itself; every man is a piece of the continent, a part of the main," as was wonderfully expressed by the poet John Donne.[76] To be concerned about one's own well-being while simultaneously providing one's service to the community is a high form of art that we can strive for with the forces of Mars.

- **Lesson 8: Superheroes can do it by themselves but are more powerful in teams.** In our time in particular, it can feel like weakness when we realize that we cannot do everything on our own. But it is impossible to do everything, really everything, on our own. And yet we keep trying. If we can jump over this shadow and ask other people for help or bring them onboard, then we can achieve a lot more. Mars as the god of war does not go into battle alone.

- **Lesson 9: Superheroes' true strengths come from their character.** Regardless of what your superpower is, your real strength comes through your personality and character. It takes a certain courage to express one's personality. If someone is shy, they can show this with benevolent restraint, instead of hiding behind vague statements. Or someone with a sunny disposition can create a friendly atmosphere instead of playing the halftime entertainer. People's characters are as diverse as their physical appearances. Truly expressed, they serve the whole.

- **Lesson 10: Superheroes perform heroic deeds.** Heroic deeds don't usually appear in the media. Heroic deeds can be found in the smallest of everyday activities. Shopping for an elderly neighbor, asking how the kiosk woman is really doing after she hasn't been there for three weeks; picking up the apples that rolled out of a stranger's basket or saving the world from destruction—nothing is too big or too small to be considered a heroic act.

With these ten lessons everyone can find their personal Superman or Wonder Woman and put their personal stamp of generosity and friendliness on the world.

Identify one of your superpowers. If you have a hard time finding one, think about what someone who knows you well might say, or something that you are often complimented on. Now go through the ten lessons above and see which ones could strengthen your superpower.

Working with Mars Forces in Daily Life: Creating a Culture of Mistakes

In 1935, a young physician named Hans Selye was on a mission to discover a new sex hormone. Strongly convinced that there was an additional hormone yet to be identified, he began preparing extracts from ovarian and placental tissues and injecting them into rats. His logic was that in doing so, he could observe the rats' reactions and look for responses that could not be attributed to the effects of the known hormones. To his excitement, he saw that his ovarian extracts *did* produce effects that could not be explained by hormones already identified: the rats developed enlarged adrenal cortexes, atrophy of lymphatic organs, and ulcerations in the gut and stomach. He was thrilled with his swift success! This joy was short-lived, however. Further testing showed that placental extracts, pituitary extracts, even extracts of completely unrelated tissues produced the same effect. Confusingly, however, the effects were diminished when he tried to purify the extracts. And then it dawned on him: Maybe he wasn't observing the effects of a new hormone—maybe he was observing the toxic effects of contaminants in his extracts. He repeated his process with formaldehyde—a toxic substance containing no tissue extracts at all. Sure enough, he observed the same set of responses. He was devastated: "I became so depressed that for a few days I could not do any work at all. I just sat in my laboratory, brooding about how this misadventure might have been avoided and wondering what was to be done now."[77]

The story does not end there, however. After picking himself up, he realized that if he viewed his results from another angle, then perhaps he had made a major discovery after all. Rather than discovering a new sex hormone as he had hoped, he'd discovered how the body responds systematically to toxic substances. He was reminded of something that had piqued his interest in medical school—how many illnesses are accompanied by the same generic set of symptoms such as achy joints, pallid skin, and digestive disturbance. His instructors taught him to disregard such symptoms because they are nonspecific to the actual illness, but now he could see that they were the outward manifestation of the body's response to being sick. In other words, these responses could provide important insights into the body's coordinated response to outside interference. He labeled this response the "general adaptation syndrome," and his work became the foundation for understanding how the body responds to stress over time.

History is full of examples of failures and accidents that later changed the world—from penicillin to Post-it® notes. They are what the late artist Bob Ross referred to as "happy accidents." As long as you stay in a frame of mind that says, "This is not the way it was supposed to go!" you remain blind to other possibilities. But when you shift your thinking to the question of, "What else can I do with this unexpected result?" then the forces of creativity are activated, and you invite in new possibilities.

It might seem counterintuitive, but mistakes are an essential component of the Mars gesture. Recall the image of the knight from earlier in the chapter—the one who never enters a battle with the certainty of success, and who would be considered cowardly if he only challenged opponents who were obviously inferior. The honor of the knight comes from the willingness to fail. Mistakes and failures in the Mars sense are always future-oriented. They are not something that ends a process, but a type of new beginning, a reorientation. When we recognize them, we can ask ourselves where this unexpected door might lead us. Or perhaps they are a test of our mettle: The setback wants to know whether you are really committed to the path you set out on. Will you press forward and try again to surmount it? Will you attempt to transform it into a victory? Parzival experienced several major failures, but each time he picked himself up from his disgrace, he recommitted to his path, righting his wrongs and fulfilling his destiny.

Rudolf Steiner described "steadfastness" as one of the qualities that students on the path of higher development must cultivate. He said,

> Nothing should lead us to abandon something we have decided upon except the insight that we have made a mistake. . . . If we act out of love we shall never tire of transforming our resolutions into deeds, no matter how often we may have failed in the past.[78]

Here we see the essential quality of Mars: Commit to a path and go for it. Keep going until you see that you've made an error. Reevaluate, adjust the path, and repeat. Mistakes and setbacks do not call into question the commitment to action, only the course those actions have taken. They are messengers that communicate that some idea or other part of our plan was out of sync with reality, or that we were carrying along something that did not serve our purpose. By creating a "culture of mistakes" (as German author and editor Wolfgang Held calls it), we can take an interest in our errors and in what they have to teach us, and we can let go once and for all of the idea that things ought to turn out just the way we planned.[79]

> Think of an accomplishment in your life that you are proud
> of. Trace it back in time to the moment that you committed
> to that goal. Now find one or two mistakes or setbacks you
> experienced along the way. How did they serve the eventual
> success of the endeavor?

Getting in the Last Word

The last word in this chapter is once again given to Mars, because another organ that Rudolf Steiner calls the quintessence of Mars is the larynx. This magical space that acts as the gatekeeper to the respiratory system is all about the kind of resistance that we have been discussing. The epiglottis and vestibular folds, for instance, prevent food or liquids from entering and causing choking. Moreover, the vocal cords use resistance to create the vibrations that are heard as sounds and allow us to produce spoken language. Everything in this area has to be regulated very strictly, otherwise you will choke or have a lump in your throat. It is the birthplace of language.

Contrary to the schoolyard adage that "words can never hurt you," language can literally be deadly. People can use violent language to provoke physical violence, as if their words are in a fistfight and complete sentences of particularly beautiful poetry cannot be formed. Instead, individual scraps of words and snorts set the scene for a targeted punch that devolves into mayhem.

Vilém Flusser, the media philosopher and communication scientist introduced earlier, described in his book *The Freedom of the Migrant:*

Objections to Nationalism that it is of the utmost importance to have a good command of your mother tongue. He said: "Anyone who loves his own mother tongue must necessarily love all other languages as well (so cannot be a nationalist), because the beauty of all languages only shines in comparison to other languages."[80]

He also said that someone who only has a weak command of their mother tongue would inevitably perceive someone who speaks differently as a threat. We can see what Flusser means with an example. Let's imagine two people get into an argument in a bar. One of them has gotten very angry and wants to punch the other, but instead says: "I'm sorry to have to tell you that my emotional situation has shifted during the last ten minutes in such a way that I think it makes sense to propel my fist into your face with a certain force." It would probably never be spoken that way. More likely, it sounds like, "Hey! What'd you say? Huh? Wanna feel some pain, jerk?" Or maybe the action proceeds before the words can even be spoken.

Who doesn't know the feeling of having words stuck in your throat? It is a sensation that's accompanied by a feeling of powerlessness. Or we find a war of words in endless debates in fruitless business or personal settings. There is talk back and forth, no resolutions are passed, and all items on the agenda are postponed to the next meeting. How beneficial it is (albeit a bit tense) when someone knocks on the table and speaks truth to power, and an agreement is finally reached. Finally! Just as words can both impede progress and create progress, words can both harm and heal. A word of honor and recognition is sometimes enough to inspire someone to perform at their best. Any business owner who has a good word for every employee creates an atmosphere of contentment and pride. Words are powerful as both sword and shield, and the one who wields them well shares in their power, as well as the responsibility for their impact. With this in mind, we close with a word to the wise: Say what you want to say and don't say what you don't want to say.

6

JUPITER

Wait a Minute

It's a familiar experience: The season changes, and you pull out the appropriate clothes from the back of the closet. You look forward to reconnecting with these loyal companions who've been patiently waiting for another day in the sun. You reach for your favorite dress and slip it on . . . Wait a minute, something's wrong here! Has the color faded? Does it no longer fit? Was this really my favorite dress last summer?

In disbelief, you consult the mirror, let your gaze wander, looking for the source of the discomfort. Slowly you realize that the problem is not with the dress, but rather with the person in the mirror. Something has changed, but what? This moment could be compared to when a snake sheds its skin or a lobster molts in order to continue growing. Somehow you have outgrown your old skin (metaphorically speaking), and you realize that a fresh layer is needed to hold the new you.

Somehow you've fallen out of time. What was right for years suddenly no longer is. This moment brings us into a space of reorientation. You need to make an update or adjustment before you can move on. Whether it is an outgrowth or an ending, each realization like this pulls us out of the flow of time momentarily and washes us into a new, empty space.

There is a similar feeling when you reach the end of a book that you've been blissfully immersed in. When you reach the end of the last line, you find yourself in a void and have to reorient yourself for a moment. A deep breath, a few moments of silence, and you can step back into the stream of time. A similar need occurs when you become aware of a habit that has actually not worked for a long time, such as still serving your soon-to-be-grown children drinks in plastic cups. It is time to put that phase to rest, get the beautiful dishes from the cellar, and enjoy this new chapter while it lasts. You are now parents of big children, and one day you will be the parent of independent adults who no longer live at home. Life invites us again and again to examine our different roles and to adjust them as necessary.

What's more, we cannot keep the skin we've grown out of and shed off. In fact, many creatures that shed their skin or shell will eat it—no sense letting all those nutrients go to waste! Sometimes this can be a painful realization, for example when we have outgrown friendships. They're still a good person, and you're still a good person, and you still like them, and yet you have the feeling that your chapter together has come to an end. You know that to hang on to the old skin would be uncomfortable and unnatural, but it's still hard to release it once and for all.

There are many reasons we need to step out of our old image of ourselves: your body has changed, your worldview has shifted, your children have left the nest, you've found your professional destiny, or suddenly you find yourself a widow. In each case, the old self has a certain inertia, but it is only a matter of time before the curtain is lifted, the spotlight is focused, and we see ourselves as if for the first time: Wait a minute! When we experience this illumination, we are free to accept the invitation and ask ourselves: Is this role still up-to-date in my life? If we see that it needs to be updated, we can shed the old skin and move on until . . . Yes, until the next moment when we are once again taken out of time and back into this space of updates and adjustment.

> Think of a time in your life when you realized something just wasn't "you" anymore. Were you able to shed this layer of skin? And, if so, how did it feel?

Solo Theater

When we set out into the world of adulthood, we find ourselves in the grand play of life. One player among many. The lead in some scenes, a supporting character in others, an extra in many more. But from around the age of 50, the curtain can open on a very special stage: that of the solo theater. We have been able to gather a lot of stage experience, so to speak, and we are now ready to use all of this knowledge for our own one-person show. So raise the curtain and begin!

Act I: You have either arrived at this phase in life with a new goal or vision from the crisis years of the 40s, or not. The latter could lead to you stubbornly holding onto your status in your job, blocking new opportunities from developing, and feeling compelled to show everyone that you are still important and that it wouldn't work without you. Father Richard Rohr refers to this orientation as the "first half of life thinking."[81] You cling to your familiar role and are afraid of change due to a lack of visionary ideas about your future. Or you might find yourself alone in a large house, with the kids moved out and your partner immersed in a meaningful career. You spend your days cleaning the house thoroughly and complaining to yourself that you get stuck with all of the work. You can taste bitterness if you arrive in your 50s with no new plan or refreshed ideas. However, there is another possibility. As the years of physical fertility come to an end, fruitful new soul and spiritual impulses can arise from it. We can awaken to what Father Rohr calls the "second half of life thinking"[82]—an opportunity for growth that comes from releasing our grasp on what we previously thought we couldn't live without.

Once you have found a goal for the new phase or a feeling that a new goal, a new focus is looming, then the first act of solo theater can really begin. We start by taking an earnest review of life. What roles have I played so far? In the mind's eye you fill the stage with these roles, letting each one pass before your gaze, and letting them sink in once again. A whole panorama opens up. You check each role by consciously slipping into the costume. Are you still the nice guy in the office, always saying yes? Are you still your children's chauffeur? The reluctant neighbor? The regular at the little cafe around the corner? The competitive athlete? The loving partner? You don't just slip into the costume, you also check whether you still feel comfortable and can identify with the role. Can you still play that part?

Act II: All kinds of roles are now standing around on the stage of the solo theater. The task now is to find out what you would like to do next with yourself and your life. The 50s can definitely be a time in life when a new creative impulse crawls in. Perhaps you will start playing the instrument you set aside thirty years ago. Or you ask yourself where you want to put your knowledge and experience to use, and how you might start to pass it on to the next generation? And where in the social sphere do you want to get involved? What do you need to reach your higher goal, your vision? With thoughts and questions like these, some roles on the stage suddenly become obsolete. You don't want to drive your kids around anymore. You have had enough of pushing yourself to the edge physically in your weekend job. A phase of sorting out begins. The roles you have outgrown, in whose skin you no longer feel comfortable, you leave behind, taking them off the stage. Perhaps you encounter small tragedies, dramas, or even comedies as you go through this process. But over time you become more courageous, honest, and intimate in bringing your solo theater piece into form.

Act III: With this second creative climax in life, you learn to let go of some obligations and delegate some tasks, creating a new space that naturally wants to be filled. So this third act is about finding out which roles are still missing. Where are you going? What do you need? With whom do you want to deepen your relationship?

During this time you not only experience a creative boost but also a certain distance from your little imperfections. It is liberating to discover that you don't have to strive for the physique of a model anymore, that your gray hair is beautiful, and that you no longer have to feel embarrassed when you forget someone's name. Feeling good in your own skin becomes much easier and is much more important. You don't *have to* anymore, you *want to*. So you examine your stage from a certain distance and look for the missing roles that need to be cast for your play to commence in earnest.

The detachment from the worldly, the desire for the social and creative, and the permission to pause for a moment are the tools to write the solo theater play. What you create no longer has to fit into a prespecified form like a tragedy, drama, or comedy because it is your stage and you are in control of how it unfolds.

What about the audience? What can they expect from this play? Ideally, they see a *person* transforming into a *personality* in all areas of his life: There is the boss who no longer feels compelled to micromanage and criticize the younger employees, but rather becomes interested in the new skills they bring and mentors them out of his experience. The neighbor has rediscovered playing the piano after a long hiatus and says hello with a joyful smile as she walks past the kitchen window. The high-performing athlete hangs up her athletic shoes and helps the elderly in the neighborhood get where they need to go. The change from being a person of society to a personality in society can take place in these years. The pace becomes more leisurely, but the forces of inspiration are picking up speed and, wait a minute: is that humor creeping back into life?

In addition to all of the roles you play, you also have been an audience member for the performances of others throughout your life. Travel back in time to your youth (prior to age 20) and think about an older person in your life (in their 50s or older) whom you admired and respected as a personality worthy of a standing ovation.

A Waltz, Not a March

Left, right, left, right, left, right, left . . . You can hear the call of the drill sergeant as the parade marches down the street. The rhythmic clip-clop of shoes is incessant, and it provides a frame that holds the ensuing music in suspense. There is no feeling of openness in this rhythm. It feels like: this, that, this, that, this, that. You feel that now you know what a ping-pong ball must feel like.

The well-known composition "Boléro" by Maurice Ravel begins with the feeling of a military march, with the familiar cadence driven by a snare drum. As the piece progresses in a strongly repetitive way, it gradually devolves into more and more chaotic sounds—horns and woodwinds and cymbal crashes, sweeping glissandi from the trombones—but never losing the driving, mechanical rhythm of the snare. During the time that he composed "Boléro," Ravel was beginning to suffer from a neurodegenerative disorder (possibly Alzheimer's disease or aphasia) that may have been connected to both the incessant rhythm of the piece and the way it grows increasingly loud and chaotic.[83, 84]

We can feel this way in life when we are confronted with polarities and polarization—left or right, pro or anti, war or peace, freedom or equality, masculine or feminine, optimism or pessimism. The conversation may start out quiet and calm, but as the voice of one side is followed by the predictable response of the other, then both positions are repeated a little more loudly because neither feels heard, and the space between grows larger rather than smaller. The "this or that" setup creates no possibility for resolution. In many contemporary groups working in the realm of diversity, equity, inclusion, or intergroup relations more generally, the term "both/and" has become a mantra. When two opposing viewpoints are presented, "both/and" invites all parties to consider the possibility that both viewpoints are true and can enrich one another, rather than the more conventional "either/or" mentality that insists that if one is right, the other is wrong. But how can we find the frame that allows for one truth not to nullify the other? Perhaps Jupiter holds some answers for us.

Terms like polarity and polarization call to mind an image of a line that is completely defined by its endpoints. "This" is on one side; "that" is on the other. When we need to somehow reconcile such opposing perspectives, the focus is often on finding the "middle ground"—the space between "this" and "that" that everyone can accept. Sometimes it's referred to as the "happy medium," but "happy" is likely a gross overstatement if everyone has given up half of what they had hoped for. The psychologist Roberto Assagioli refers to this space as *compromise*.[85] For instance, the compromise between sympathy and antipathy is something like indifference or ambivalence. The compromise does not build strength because it remains in the flatness of the polarity. In order to find a solution with the strength of sustainability, you must rise above the surface level and find a *synthesis* of the poles—one that takes a higher perspective to see how both can be true and add value to one another. Instead of indifference, we have what Assagioli called "benevolent understanding" as a higher perspective on sympathy and antipathy.[86] With this Jupiter gesture of stepping back, now the full picture, the panorama, can appear before you. This stepping back (or rising above) also defuses the emotional tension that comes with being attached to one pole or the other. Suddenly you can see your own standpoint with the same objectivity as the other.

When we work with polarities, we always look for the third that brings harmony to the opposites. The flat line becomes a triangle—the strongest and most resilient structural form. The march becomes a waltz—one, two, three; one, two, three—that gracefully adjusts its course and flows around obstacles that appear in its path. And the sound of the footsteps fades away as the newfound levity of the situation keeps the feet barely kissing the floor.

Suppostabees

We all know that voice in our heads. It says, "You should do this," "You shouldn't do that." Perhaps you give it a name like "conscience" or "moral compass" or "responsibility." However you make sense of it, the message is clear: there are right and wrong ways of being. There are thoughts you should think and ones you shouldn't. There are right feelings and wrong feelings. There are ways you should act and ways you shouldn't. There are even goals and aspirations you should have and ones you shouldn't. All of these shoulds can put a lot of weight on your shoulders that you have to lug around with you. We call these internalized ideas about how you are supposed to be *suppostabees*.

Of course these suppostabees have some social value—they help establish and maintain certain social contracts that make social life work. It's a good thing that people don't routinely solve their problems with physical violence or steal the things they want from others. However, these internalized suppostabees create expectations that can sometimes go too far, creating confusion and sowing doubt in one's ability to make decisions independently. For instance, anyone who has become a new parent (particularly mothers who have gone through pregnancy) has likely been hit from all sides with advice on the "right way" to do it, from diet to diapering to discipline. It's a dizzying experience that in the end leads to one of a few characteristic responses. On the one hand, you could throw up your hands and admit that you don't know what to think or do anymore. On the other hand, you could conclude that you just have to do it your own way.

In other cases, we acquire suppostabees more unconsciously, often as part of a cultural narrative. For instance, we implicitly learn from an early age that boys and girls should dress, act, and relate to others in different ways. We get rewarded in more or less direct ways for meeting those expectations and punished for falling short of them. By the time we become adults, we've internalized them as part of who we are. We are good to the extent that we meet these expectations and bad to the extent that we deviate from them.

This sensitivity to the expectations of others may have very deep roots. In psychology, there is a theory called "sociometer theory" that says that self-esteem—our sense of self-worth—comes from our relational value—the extent to which others like us and see us as valuable members of the group. The theorists use an evolutionary argument to suggest that in our distant past, individuals could not survive on their own, and thus being accepted and valued by others was a precondition for survival.[87] We therefore became highly attuned to this sense of social acceptance and internalized it as self-esteem.

In the Mercury chapter, we related how during childhood, expectations from others such as parents and teachers can form *conditions of worth* that shape our choices in socially desirable ways. The psychologist Carl Rogers suggested that the major problem with such conditions is that they stand in opposition to the process of *self-actualization* (the pursuit of one's own unique potential).[88] In other words, in many situations we must choose whether to follow our own hearts or to conform to these internalized expectations. Countless examples throughout history—from writers like James Joyce to innovators like Louis Pasteur—show that those who are ultimately remembered for their greatness are those who found a way to overcome their suppostabees and live out of their own deeper knowing.

The most insidious form of suppostabees may be the ones that we create to avoid choosing for ourselves. For instance, we might say, "This means a lot to them, so I should just go along with their idea," or "She's really busy, so I shouldn't tell her that she got my order wrong." These are insidious not only because we have created them ourselves (i.e., nobody taught us or asked us to be this way), but also because we give ourselves an ego boost by acting on them. They show that we are "sensitive to others' needs," that we are "selfless," that we are willing to "sacrifice" ourselves for the sake of others. However, if we take the word "sacrifice" in its original sense—to make holy—then we can see that these kinds of acts are anything but.

How do we understand these self-created suppostabees? As a starting point, the psychologist Erich Fromm described the European experience in the transition from the Middle Ages to the Modern Era.[89] In former times, all aspects of life were dictated by higher powers—the monarchy, the church, one's station in life. And then suddenly there was choice. Who should be chosen as the leader? What do I believe, and how do I worship? What will I choose as my vocation? The ability to choose is connected to the idea of freedom, but it can also be a terrifying and paralyzing experience. What if I make the wrong choice? What if I fail? What if others disapprove of my choices? The realization that one has to decide on one's own and own their decisions (for better or worse) is central to the existential dilemma and can give rise to an existential crisis. According to Fromm, one way that some people coped with their newfound freedom was by clinging to authority and hierarchy—developing over time into what he called the *authoritarian personality*.[90]

To existential philosophers like Jean-Paul Sartre, we confront questions like these (at least unconsciously) every moment of the day.[91] Every situation presents a choice of whether and how to engage it. When we withdraw from the moment, defer to authorities, let things happen as they will, leave it up to fate, or allow others to choose for us, we are acting in *bad faith*. From the existentialist perspective, by living in bad faith we forfeit our opportunity to really live and create meaning in the world out of the fear of being wrong or getting hurt. It doesn't matter whether we have concocted a self-serving explanation for not choosing. Moreover, we can only have the illusion of not choosing—in the immortal words of Geddy Lee: "If you choose not to decide, you still have made a choice."[92] The alternative is to develop *optimistic toughness* and engage every situation to its fullest in spite of the fact that we don't have all of the information, in spite of the fact that we might be wrong, and in spite of the fact that we have to own our decisions either way. It's a tall order, but by letting go of these (real and imagined) suppostabees, we will find that every day presents new opportunities for becoming more of ourselves.

Qualities of Jupiter

Jupiter is the largest and heaviest planet in our solar system. Its diameter is twelve times that of the Earth, and its weight is two and a half times as much as all the other planets in the solar system combined. After the Sun, Moon, and Venus, it is the brightest point of light in the sky. A Jupiter day lasts just ten hours as it rotates once around its axis. Consequently, its atmosphere is somewhat deformed—it is thicker at the equator than at the poles. It takes almost twelve years for Jupiter to orbit the Sun. With impressive parameters like these, Jupiter has well earned its name, since Jupiter was the king of the gods in Roman mythology.

Now, of course, the supreme deity also has a special obligation to the masses, which Jupiter the planet fulfills perfectly. Due to its incredible size, it forms an essential component of the mass equilibrium in the solar system. Jupiter (along with its neighbor Saturn) has a stabilizing effect on the asteroid belt. In fact, without Jupiter, life on Earth (and possibly the Earth itself) would likely not exist. Statistically speaking, an asteroid would escape from the asteroid belt and hit the Earth every 100,000 years, which would certainly put a damper on our party. Jupiter's gravitational pull, like a vacuum cleaner, ensures that the asteroid belt stays properly cinched. He even adds an occasional outlier to his collection of moons, which currently number eighty.

The liver, as the quintessential Jupiter organ, takes on a similar role as protector. In Chinese medicine it is called *the general*. The liver takes everything that is ingested and decides what serves the organism and what is potentially harmful and must be eliminated. Tin—the metal of Jupiter—is also necessary for the balance between the opposites, be it between liquid and solid in bones and joints or between left and right in the two hemispheres of the brain. Tin brings the opposites into equilibrium so they serve each other and enable us to gain knowledge and lead a self-determined life.

Jupiter is a guardian of the present, as opposed to the past or future. One treasure it holds for the present lies hidden in the contradictions of Jupiter. It combines speed with slowness, massiveness with responsiveness, volatility with calmness. But what is the present anyway? The present is the point of passage from future to past, and it passes very quickly. Nevertheless, the present is also eternal—it is the only time in which we can shape our lives. The past is done, the future is still out of reach. All we have is the present. And this linear time does not last either. It walks on mercilessly, and what happens in a fraction of a second can have the greatest consequences. You could almost get the feeling that you are defenseless in dealing with the present. To avoid this feeling, we may eagerly plan the future and lament about missed opportunities in the past. And somehow we do not notice that we are filling the present with clutter from other time zones. It is light and easy to dream into the future and linger on in the past; it is heavy to stay focused in the here and now. It's an almost universal experience these days to have one's head full of things that we still have to do, or things that we should have done. Dragging along this scrap heap of time in the present pushes us away from the real feeling of who we are.

The gift we get from Jupiter is to be able to add some spatial qualities to the present moment. With mindfulness and awareness, we can bring attention to the present and declutter it for a moment of all that has been or will be. A necessary space is created that allows us to step back. Wait a minute: what's going on *right now*? The view widens and an understanding of the current situation can be gained. So you look to the left and right before you cross the street and don't step carelessly into traffic. Is everything still there? Anybody missing? Do I have everything I need to start cooking? Window closed? Light off? Check, check, check. Then you get back into the flow of time and act with a sense of calmness.

Jupiter has the quality of keeping track of things peacefully and intervening at lightning speed if necessary. A child slips from her chair and we just manage to catch her before she falls, or a student almost pours the wrong liquid into the beaker, and we stop him just in time. Reacting lickety-split from a state of calm and returning back into calmness is a gift that we get from this gas giant. In this way you also learn that in an emergency you first pause to get an overview of the situation, and then you dial the emergency number. Carrying your worries and regrets with you into a situation creates a nervous energy that clouds your vision and hampers your responsiveness.

Rudolf Steiner speaks of Jupiter as the thinker among the planets. One can come to wisdom through the quality of thought. There are times when we think about a problem and we just don't get to the bottom of it, then Jupiter reaches out and helps. Here's how Steiner explains it:

> Human beings who have tried hard to apply clear thinking to some problem but cannot get to the root of it, will find, if they are patient and work inwardly at it, that the Jupiter powers will actually help them during the night. And many as one who have found a better solution for some problem during the night, as though out of dream, than during the previous day, would have to admit, if they knew the truth, that it is the Jupiter powers who imbue human thinking with mobility and vigor.[93]

At the end of the day, Jupiter not only gives us the ability to step out of time for a moment, but also gives us the night as a space where some thoughts we worked on with serious effort during the day can find resolution. "Wait a minute! I think you should sleep on it!"

As mentioned, Jupiter was the king of the gods in Roman mythology whose Greek counterpart was Zeus. Both were considered the gods of the sky and thunder, and their most recognizable symbols were the eagle and the thunderbolt. These characteristics conjure the image of one who has clear vision from a higher perspective and effective action from a distance. The eagle was also the most important symbol in the *taking of auspices* (or interpretation of omens), such that the behaviors of eagles were taken to be the most indicative of what was to come because the eagle communicated on behalf of Jupiter. In the political realm, Jupiter (also known as Jove) was the god who presided over the swearing of oaths, and the expression "by Jove" is a relic of this ancient practice.

Worship of Jupiter was central to life in ancient Rome. The Romans maintained a regular schedule of ritual sacrifices in his honor, and in exchange they believed that Jupiter blessed them with protection and support and was directly responsible for the sustained success of the Roman Empire. The arrangement contributes to the image of Jupiter as the benevolent king. Indeed, when we think about the qualities of an effective ruler, we can imagine one who has all the time in the world because he sets the pace. There is no haste for the king when he requires counsel or contemplation, and this spaciousness that he creates holds the potential for decisive action when the moment arrives. Finally, those born under the sign of Jupiter in ancient Rome were considered to be good-hearted and jolly—that is, jovial. In everyday life, those we might characterize as jovial are ones who are not overburdened by worries about the future or failures of the past. Rather, they find themselves experiencing life in the present moment, enjoying good food, immersing themselves in conversation, and taking in new experiences.

Wait a Minute—There Are a Few Rules

By now it's clear that this gesture of *Wait a Minute* is part of Jupiter's superpower. But you might be thinking, "I know someone who is always saying 'Wait a minute,' and it drives me bonkers!" So let's take a step back and find some clarity. We all know the colleague who comes to meetings, maybe a little late, a little unprepared, a little disorganized, and keeps interrupting the flow with "Wait a minute. Where are we? Can you repeat that? Was that in the proposal?" Or the person who has a hundred questions about an issue that was already discussed and then worked through by a subcommittee. "Have you kept an eye on the processes? What budget did you start from? You know she doesn't like flowers? Did you think of the vegans? Wait a minute, did you think of inviting the mother-in-law? Did you buy parsley too? Did you think about the insurance? Did you order a bus big enough for everyone? . . ."

"YEEESSSS! WE DID! BECAUSE THAT WAS ALL DISCUSSED LAST TIME!!!"

Being held up can be incredibly annoying and is not at all the quality we are talking about here. It's not about throwing Wait a Minute into the ring just because you came unprepared or are anxious about moving forward. The momentum of Wait a Minute is by no means a constant interruption.

But what is it then? Well, first of all, there is a personal Wait a Minute and a social Wait a Minute. Both arise in a similar way, but they have a different feeling and expression. In both cases, there is an interest in the big picture, a fine voice that awakens you from within, a clear thinking, and perhaps a pinch of courage. In the personal Wait a Minute, we might find ourselves being pulled along by the current of life, making decisions before we feel ready, keeping the momentum going forward but without clarity of purpose. Here, Wait a Minute interrupts this flow and steps out of the stream momentarily: *Am I thinking clearly, or am I blinded by my preconceptions or wishful thinking? Am I missing anything relevant to my decision? Must I decide now, or might it be advantageous to wait until I learn more?* We can feel the tension in this gesture—life wants to plow ahead, and it takes real effort to stand your ground—like trying to keep your kayak in one place in a flowing river.

The social Wait a Minute requires more boldness. It wants to recalibrate a situation; something new needs to be seen and taken seriously for the benefit of the collective. Or it wants to inject a reflective pause before a hasty decision that could have dire consequences. Courage is needed here because you may be met initially with sighs of frustration, so addictive is the desire for progress, but a true Wait a Minute buoys your courage because it arises from a deeper knowing.

So it can be that literally seconds before Christmas you drag yourself into town to buy a small present for all the adult guests coming to visit. The shops are full of nervous and stressed people who are planning something similar at the very last minute. But then you suddenly stop. *Wait a minute, what am I doing? Last year we decided to stop buying gifts for the adults.* This realization and a pinch of courage can lead to a satisfying outbreath and letting go of the whole nerve-wracking search. In the end, you might be the only one who comes to Christmas dinner without a present for the adults, but then you say, "Wait a minute, last year we decided not to buy any more presents!" And so it can happen that next year everyone can exhale and enjoy a more relaxed holiday season.

Finally, there are other times when Wait a Minute is an inner calling to get out of the way. Many of us have an inclination to hold tightly onto projects that matter a lot to us, particularly ones where we're in a leadership position. Part of the lesson of Jupiter is that to be a leader does not always mean being out front and claiming responsibility for victory. Some of the best leadership moments can arise when you realize that the team knows what they need to do and has the skills to make it happen. They've worked it through, considered the ramifications of the different possibilities, and have a clear plan. They work well together, communicate with you and with each other clearly. In those moments, Wait a Minute allows you to see that everything is under control and that the best way for you to serve the goal is to become a support, a shepherd, a steward, or a mentor.

Working with Jupiter Forces in Daily Life: Becoming Completely Imperfect

The book *The Professor and the Madman* by Simon Winchester details the process by which the original Oxford English Dictionary came into being in the nineteenth century. Professor James Murray led a team that was tasked with compiling and defining every word in the English language for the first time ever.[94] What an enormous undertaking! In fact, it was an impossible task. They had to solicit, receive, organize, resolve discrepancies, consolidate, assemble, and proof every English language word from 1150 AD onward at the same time that the language continued to develop and evolve in various countries around the world. How could they even know when their task was done? And how could they bring themselves to send it to the printer, knowing that they were undoubtedly missing some (possibly many) words? And yet if they never crossed that threshold and the dictionary was never published, the project would have gone down in history as a colossal waste of time and resources. Here, committing to perfection would have been a deathblow for the project.

While this might be an extreme example in terms of the scope of a project, we can find many examples from daily life where perfectionism becomes a barrier to progress. Where can we find a counterpart to perfection that encourages rather than hinders forward movement? The answer may be found in the number twelve, which as we've seen has a special connection to Jupiter. Throughout history and across many cultures, the number twelve has represented completion and a natural way of dividing a whole into parts. For instance, there are twelve full lunar cycles in a solar year, with a bit left over. The convention of dividing the day into twelve hours dates back approximately five thousand years to the Sumerian civilization. The Sumerians used a base-60 number system (think minutes and seconds), and twelve is one-fifth of 60. Both of these numbers have well-established properties that make them easy to work with, such as being divisible by many numbers (a property not shared by our modern base-10 system). Interestingly, though, because the twelve hours of the day were equally divided between sunrise and sunset (being measured by "shadow clocks"), the length of an hour varied depending on your location and the time of year. Complete, but not perfect. In the Bible, Jesus chose twelve apostles to carry forward his mission, one of whom (Judas Iscariot) ultimately betrayed him to the authorities. And there are twelve astrological signs evenly spread across the year, even though the corresponding constellations differ in size. Again, complete, but not perfect.

"Complete" says: "Everything needed to move forward is present." We may need to start the journey with what we have, find out what is lacking as we go, and adjust the course as needed. The shadow clocks whose hours varied seasonally served a purpose that later mechanical clocks (which didn't depend on the sun) could improve upon. Neither clocks were (or are) perfect, but both represent a completion—the allowing of an activity to come to an end, to be released. We can draw another example out of everyday experience. Imagine that you take a jigsaw puzzle off of the shelf and open it up. It is not apparent at first glance whether all 1,000 pieces are present or whether one or two might be missing. The gesture of perfection would require confirmation that nothing is missing before getting started, while the gesture of completion would say that we have what we need to move forward. Likewise, when you approach the end and realize that there are a few missing pieces, the gesture of perfection would put everything else on hold until those last pieces are found and put into place, while the gesture of completion would feel satisfied that all of the pieces in the box had been assembled and would be open to whatever was to come next. Sure, there might be a tinge of disappointment about the missing pieces, but it shouldn't break the flow of activity.

A common way that perfectionism presents itself is as procrastination. On the surface, procrastination might seem like the opposite of perfection—if you want something to be perfect, why would you delay getting started? But it is precisely this need for perfection that can prevent the first step from being taken. Or, to turn this relationship around, perfectionism can sometimes be a crutch or excuse arising out of fear of what comes next. To draw another literary analogy, in the book *Wonder Boys* by Michael Chabon, the main character is an aging writer working on his masterpiece. The problem is he just can't bring it to an end. The story goes on and on and on, filling thousands of pages with no end in sight. He's not procrastinating in his writing, but in bringing the work to a close.[95] Because then what? What if it's a flop? How else will he spend his time? How else can he continue to justify his neglect of other responsibilities? So here we see the striving for perfection as an expression of a fear of what happens after the end.

The truth is that moving forward in spite of imperfection requires a healthy dose of vulnerability. The lobster has no choice but to molt as it outgrows its old shell, but once it does, its new soft shell leaves it more vulnerable to predators for several months. In contrast to the lobster, we have more self-awareness of the vulnerability and the risks associated with stepping out of the old ways that no longer fit, and we have choices about what to do with this awareness. The power of

Jupiter and the Wait A Minute impulse provide us with the tools we need to see the situation from a higher perspective. We can see that the old ways are connected to a version of ourselves that is no longer there; we need to let go of the old and welcome the new to serve the present version of ourselves.

A Snake, an Actor, and a Suppostabee Walk into a Bar . . .

(Snake and Actor walk in and take a seat at the bar.)

Actor: Oh, Snake, I'm so thankful for your advice. The spa was wonderful, and the skin care was beyond measure. I've never been exfoliated like that before. I feel like a new person.

Snake: My pleasure! I'm kind of an expert in that domain.

Bartender *(to Snake)*: The usual?

Snake: You bet.

Bartender *(to Actor)*: How about you?

Actor: I'll have a Tom Collins.

Bartender *(to Actor)*: Coming right up.

(Suppostabee walks in, lets out a sigh of annoyance.)

Suppostabee: You know, you really should put up a better sign—I almost missed the place. And sorry I'm late—my boss should learn to let us go on time. I can't stay long. I'm supposed to be home already. I really shouldn't have too much to drink.

Bartender *(to Suppostabee)*: Hello to you, too. What can I get you?

Suppostabee: I don't know—what do you think I should have? What do people like me usually order?

Bartender *(to Suppostabee)*: Well, I don't know what kind of people you are. Maybe you want to start with a glass of water while you think it over?

Suppostabee: Shouldn't you offer me a proper drink? Isn't that your job?

Bartender *(to Suppostabee)*:   Alright then, what kind of drink do you like?

Suppostabee: Well, I like sour drinks, but I shouldn't have them because of my ulcer. And I like sweet drinks too, but I shouldn't have too much sugar. I don't really like the taste of red wine, but someone told me it's healthy, so maybe I should have a red wine . . .

Snake: I'm gonna need a second round.

Bartender *(to Snake)*: You got it.

Bartender *(to Actor)*: Can I get you something else too?

Actor: Maybe another Tom Collins.

Suppostabee: Hey, that's rude. You're supposed to serve me before you get them another round.

Bartender *(to Suppostabee)*: Sure. Did you decide what you want?

Suppostabee: No, but . . .

Bartender *(to Actor)*: Wait a minute! Now I know who you are. You're the actor from that old TV show. A Tom Collins was always your drink on the show too. How about stepping out of the old role and trying something new?

Actor: Hmmmm . . . sure. Actually, I've always wanted to try a Sazerac. I just like the sound of it: Sssssazerac. Can you make me one of those?

Bartender *(to Actor)*: Great choice.

Suppostabee: Oh well, looks like everyone has what they need, except for poor little me.

Bartender *(to Suppostabee)*: Okay, last chance. What's it going to be?

Suppostabee: You're the bartender. You should know.

Bartender *(to Suppostabee)*: Look, if you don't know what you want, maybe you should go home and figure it out yourself.

Suppostabee: You expect me to go all the way home to Mill Street, and then come back here for a drink?

Snake *(to Suppostabee)*: You know what, I'm heading the same direction. Why don't we share a cab? My skin is thick enough to bear your company.

Suppostabee: Whatever. I'm supposed to be home anyway.

(Snake and Suppostabee walk out.)

(Actor slips Bartender $100)

Actor: You can keep the change—one good tip deserves another. Thanks for helping me realize I need to step out of my old role and go for something new. It was exactly what I needed, right here, right now. I feel complete.

Bartender: Perfect. My pleasure.

(Actor walks out)

7

SATURN

The Courage to Die and the Fear to Become

"Try to stay present." We often hear advice like this, and perhaps we often repeat it to ourselves as well. It's advice that says: "Focus on what is happening right here, right now . . . Bring your attention to your current field of activity." Well, not to discount the importance of presence, in this chapter we're going to tuck the present away for a while and live into its necessary companions of past and future. The present is where these two companions meet and enter into conversation. Sometimes they get along well, sometimes they clash, and sometimes their encounter is indecipherable. Both past and future have the ability to captivate us, and perhaps each of us is more prone to one than the other—ruminating on events of the past or worrying about the future. Where do these lead us? When in our lives does it serve us to step into one realm or the other?

Upon first glance, we might say that past and future differ in their knowableness and their mutability. The past has already happened, and what has happened is knowable; we either hold it in our experience already, or we can do some investigating and find out. We also have the sense, then, that the past is immutable. It cannot be changed any more than lead can be changed into gold. "What is done is done." And it's this apparent fixedness of the past that we can get caught up in.

In contrast, when we look toward the future, it can seem as if a veil or curtain stands before us. We don't know what is behind the curtain, and perhaps we even imagine that the set dressers and cast are constantly rearranging things until the moment the curtain goes up. Although we can anticipate (or predict or forecast) certain aspects of the future, it seems otherwise unknowable until it appears before us. So when we look toward the future, it is this uncertainty that can draw us in. "It's anyone's guess."

But when you look back at the past, what do you see? Do you see a string of unrelated coincidences, or do you see a fabric of interwoven experiences, encounters, successes, and setbacks? With storytelling as deeply rooted in the human condition as it is, the chances are good that you see interconnections, cause-and-effect relationships, and the manifestation of your beliefs about yourself and the world. It seems only logical that the past would have this kind of coherence, and we often look to the past when we have questions about a current situation. Here, the exceptions may make the rule—with certain events standing out because they just don't fit the general picture you've developed. So we can say that the past is *researchable*—we can look to the past to unravel different connections and correlations and gain new insights. Of course, we have no obligation to undertake such a project—

instead, we may choose to "let bygones be bygones" and leave the past behind us.

But what about the future? Does it make sense to think about the future as researchable too? Are we being pushed into the future by the past? If so, it should suggest that the uncertainty of the future is primarily due to our incomplete knowledge of the past—if only we could grasp all of the details, we could be sure of what is coming. Alternatively, does the future stream toward us, bringing with it new ideas, new contingencies, and new possibilities that do not follow from the stream of the past? If so, how can we learn to listen to what the future is speaking to us? In other words, is the future a becoming or a coming? Here again we can bring in the two conceptions of the future from the philosopher Stefan Brotbeck.[96]

If the future is a becoming, then it represents the unfolding of prospects that are inherent from the origin, be this a person, a thing, or the laws of nature—just as the flower develops from a seed. In Latin, the word *futurum* is used to describe this forward direction of time. Since the future is to be found in the existing possibility, this *futurum* can be understood as an extension of the past and present. You can plan it in advance with a greater or lesser verisimilitude. The scientific study of the future is called *futurology* or *futures studies* and can be defined as follows:

> Futures studies are the scientific study of possible, desirable, and probable future developments and scope for design, as well as the conditions for these in the past and in the present. Modern futures studies assume that the future is not entirely determinable and that different future developments ("futures") are possible and there is scope for design. They are based on

the realization that there are indeed a great number of possible futures but that these are not arbitrary.[97]

This science of predicting the future is present across many important domains, from climate change to the rise of political movements to changes in the economy, and the rise of "big data," artificial intelligence, and powerful computing technologies allow more and more past and present conditions to be incorporated into the models. We see in the definition that there is acknowledgment that the future is not entirely knowable, but that the possible futures are constrained by what we know about the past.

If the future is a coming, then the Latin term *adventus* applies. This future stream comes toward the present from the future and represents a counterforce to the past. It can be seen as a large space where visions and expectations can unfold. In other words, it refers to possibilities being prepared for us that we cannot yet fully know or understand. Have you ever had the strong feeling that you have to do something, even though the source of the impulse and the potential consequences are not yet clear? Did you always know that you would like to live in Kyrgyzstan one day? Has a certain language captivated you, so you learned it even though you didn't know anyone who spoke it? Where do such ideas come from? Might they be whispering invitations from a future that wants to come into being? What would it be like if we could train our sense of listening to learn the language of the future? For example, in the time before women gained the right to vote, a movement developed around this idea. A new language had to be created to express the need for a future that would be a break from the past, and now we can no longer imagine a present that does not include women's suffrage. Something that now seems obvious and inevitable was at one time unimaginable. Where did the impulse of such a movement come from?

We see (as we described in the Sun chapter) that there are two orientations toward the future—the *futurum* streaming from the past and the *adventus* arising out of new possibilities—and we come to know ourselves and the world better as we can connect with both of them in our present moments. Can we also find another side to the past? Is there any way that the past lives in the future? In some ways, this question is fundamental to biography and social art work, and we explore it in more detail later in this chapter. For the moment, however, we'll simply hold the idea that not all past experiences can be readily incorporated into the otherwise coherent story of our lives. Why did she look at me that way? Why didn't he show up? Of all the times for my car to not start, why this time? These moments can sometimes be turning points in life, and we may hold questions like these for many years until one day when something unexpected happens and it suddenly makes sense. As the country music star Garth Brooks sings, "some of God's greatest gifts are unanswered prayers."[98]

Think about a time when someone came into your life unexpectedly and had a profound impact on you. Perhaps you experienced an immediate feeling of connection, or maybe they said exactly what you needed to hear in that moment. What journey did that encounter take you on that would not otherwise have happened?

Sorting Out Affairs

Of course we are always living at the interface of these worlds—past, present, and future. But we become more acutely aware of them at certain moments of life that we might call *thresholds*. A threshold marks a boundary between spaces, but it is more than merely a dividing line. Typically, one of these spaces is more familiar, more full of light, and the other is more unknown, less illuminated, and the movement is from the familiar into the unknown.

As individuals approach the end of their work life, a new realm lies beyond the horizon. In some ways, this post-employment life holds all of the possibilities of living freely—achieving unfulfilled goals, pursuing long-held dreams, and checking items off of one's "bucket list." On the other hand, this time is also marked by new questions and challenges.

Just as we don't wish someone who is young to live without a meaningful future, we should not wish someone who is old to live without a meaningful past. How does this happen, and what does it look like? The acquired past is a kind of fabric in which all events, encounters, and stories of one's own life have been artfully interwoven. You can look at it superficially or dive into the depths and try to recover the treasure. But what's the point of this? It's over and you can't change it anymore! But just as we support young people at the beginning of their working life to actively step into an uncertain future and not just passively let themselves be carried along by events, so when the scale shows more past than future in our lives, we should also actively deal with what we have been and done. How does it feel when nobody listens, when you are not seen, and your own story cannot be told?

The events of the past are irrevocably over, like a book that has been written. The words are stored between the book covers and will never change again. But the moment you have the courage to open the book, the story can unfold, and you can discover various secrets, thus creating an inner journey that can become fuller and fuller in the time of life when outer life forces are receding. With curiosity we might find dramas, comedies, action, and all other kinds of plays in it.

Courageous powers are required here. Whereas early in life, courageous forces were needed for the conquest of the future, in this phase of life they lie in looking with courage into the past. What could you come across? Small connections may become clear, events that happened independently of one another may lead to an important step in your biography. Perhaps you will also find painful things. An argument that was never resolved or an insult that was never apologized for. A courageous look into the past can lead us to put things in order, to make a clean sweep. It takes courage to look into the past because it can represent the death of the future. The future and all its possibilities have, so to speak, died into the fixedness of the past.

So we need courage to die. The fear in this stage of life can be marked by the inevitability of death—although it may be many years away, its presence grows stronger. We would like to pack everything we ever wanted to do in this last phase. We want a lot, and slowly we can physically do less. This can fuel tremendous fears. Delaying aging also leads to death in the end. But what else can fear do besides paralyze and freeze us? In the early years, fear might have appeared when we left home, studied in another city, or went traveling alone for the first time, but it always led us to action. Something took place outside that we encountered with our own actions. In old age, the outside changes to the inside and the inside to the outside. Now is the time when we find wealth inside and slowly in our outer life we transfer from a human doer to a human being. You don't have to do anything anymore, you just are. The present gains in duration, the past grows in size, and the future comes like a gentle gust of wind from the near distance.

To have the courage to die and the fear to become means, in this phase of life, to clear up the past, to sort out one's affairs as broadly as possible. To bring conversations that are still open to an end, to reach out to people with whom there are still unresolved issues, or maybe to organize your library, read old love letters again, listen to the children, and find a place where your own story can be told. Whether or not we can face death more easily in this way remains to be seen, but fear and courage will be by our side.

Regrets . . . I've Had a Few

When you look back at your life so far, hopefully there are moments that stand out where you are really proud of yourself: You did something bold or courageous. You spoke up for someone with less power. You worked hard until you achieved a challenging goal. Or maybe you're proud of some moments where you held yourself back—You *didn't* say or do something that might have felt good in the moment but would have been hurtful to someone else or your future self. However, the chances are good that there are also moments that you're not proud of: careless mistakes, hurtful actions, missed opportunities, and unkind words. When such moments come to mind, it can be easy to slide into the mode of regret.

The word *regret* has been around since the fourteenth century in connection with grief: weeping or bewailing someone's death, possibly long after the loss.[99] There is a sense of longing, pain, and distress associated with regret, possibly because of the reality of not being able to turn back the hands of time and change the actions of the past.

We can experience regret with respect to things said and done (what psychologists sometimes call errors of action or commission) as well as those things *not* said or done (errors of inaction or omission). In either case, regret develops in the wake of the incident, as the impact and irreversibility of the incident becomes clear. Psychologists Tom Gilovich and Victoria Medvec, who wrote a seminal review on the psychology of regret, refer to regret as a kind of "felt-reason or reasoned-emotion"[100] —that is a feeling infused with thinking, particularly thoughts about how other courses of actions would have led to more favorable results. There may also be a sense that you should have known better—that you were capable of taking the preferable course of action, but you didn't, whether it was due to carelessness, being overwhelmed by emotion, or some other reason. In other words, you might experience regret if you get pulled over for speeding on the way to an important meeting and end up being too late, but probably not if you'd been late because you were lost trying to get to someplace you never saw before in the dark and rain. The first was totally avoidable, while the latter, while unfortunate, can more easily be attributed to outside factors. You don't have to shoulder the blame entirely on your own.

Interestingly, Gilovich and Medvec report that regret shifts over time. When people are asked what the most regrettable moments of their lives have been, the majority point to inactions. However, when their attention is focused on the shorter term, errors of action weigh more heavily. Gilovich and Medvec suggest a number of psychological explanations for this transformation. For instance, because the consequences of faulty actions are felt more strongly right away, people may be more likely to take action to remedy the situation, whereas the consequences of inaction tend to become apparent and grow stronger only over time, at which point repair work may be more difficult. Similarly, whereas the consequences of poor actions are clear and concrete, inactions tend to lend themselves more to the imagination of "the life that might have been." Regardless of the exact process, individuals in their twilight years often report more regret over inactions than actions.

Is there a point to experiencing regret? And is there a way to transform errors into learning experiences without enduring feelings of regret? Some brain imaging work suggests that regret experiences are reactivated in later situations as part of a *regret avoidance* process.[101] In other words, people may get a mental reminder of the aversiveness of past errors that cue them to be more careful in later situations. So regret may be a component of a learning process designed to help improve future decisions and future outcomes. This sounds reasonable in the short term, but long-term regrets (such as those still present in the elder years) seem to be less adaptive. They draw us out of the present and back into the past, dwelling on the turning points that defined our course through life, for better or worse. As "felt reason or reasoned emotions," regrets can commandeer our thinking and hinder our ability to fully experience the life in front of us.

Regret is linked to our desire for control and belief in self-determination. If only I had paid more attention, or acted more carefully, or thought it through more, or held myself back, things would have turned out so much better. In our stories of our lives, we are the center of the action, and we tend to hold ourselves accountable for carrying the plot. Our imaginations run wild, creating an image of the parallel universe that we could have lived in. With that type of mindset, regret is almost inevitable. However, if we can step out of our own story for a moment, we find that we are not at the center at all. We are one of myriad moving parts in a vastly complex system, much of which is completely out of our control. Even within ourselves, we likely overestimate how much we can control our thoughts, feelings, and actions. This does not make us flawed, but rather it makes us human. And as we stand outside of ourselves, seeing ourselves as one of many characters in this grand play, we may begin to recognize the hidden gold of our past mistakes: the people we wouldn't have met or allowed ourselves to get close to; the lessons that we might not have been able to learn any other way; the challenges we wouldn't have known we could overcome; the motivation to persevere at something, knowing that we've been through worse. From this vantage point, we may even begin to develop a measure of gratitude for our past failures, seeing the quiet richness they've brought into our lives. And from the place of gratitude, perhaps we can begin to release ourselves from the bonds of the past and see the life of potential that lies before us. We are not our past mistakes, but our life would not be our life without them.

Qualities of Saturn

Saturn marks the outermost planet of the classical solar system and closes it off from the outer cosmos. Of course, the most distinctive feature of Saturn is its rings, which form a kind of belt around its middle. In both of these respects, we can see that Saturn has a quality of boundaries and containment. In our chapter on the Moon, we discussed the concealed inner aspect in relation to its visible outer aspect. With Saturn, it is the reverse: What is inside is known, while what lies beyond is somehow "other" and mysterious. With its orbital period of almost thirty years, Saturn is also the slowest of the classical planets. Since it can be seen with the naked eye, it has had a meaning in every culture. It takes its name from the Roman god Saturnus, the god of agriculture. Saturn was identified with the Greek titan Kronos.

Lead is the metal that belongs to Saturn. With the understanding of the qualities of lead, we can recognize the full power of Saturn and experience some surprises. For one thing, lead looks dull and gray, it looks heavy and cold. If we can hold a lump of lead in our hands, the heaviness is confirmed, but not the cold. Lead is a surprisingly warm metal. Warmth is an essential quality in life; without warmth there would be no life. It is also the basis for an interest in the other person. We notice this in the saying: to give someone the cold shoulder. So, we can say that our planetary system is held by warmth at the outer edge. Where do we find warmth around the outer edge in our lives? Where would we like to experience it? Can an embrace be a little Saturn gesture in our daily lives?

Another quality of lead is that it is an extremely soft metal. You can scratch it with your fingernail. We use this quality, for example, when we want to examine explosives. You let the explosion happen in a lead cylinder and then you can see the imprints—because the lead absorbed the impact without being destroyed. The imprint is permanent.

In ourselves we have this quality of imprinting in our life stories. With our ability to remember we can bring them to our consciousness. What does it take to not be overwhelmed by all the sensory impressions we take in? It requires the quality of lead to kill the living sensory impressions to such an extent that they no longer seem overwhelming. Rudolf Steiner says:

> . . . this fine lead substance works on human beings. . . . They (the students) knew that our sense organs, especially the organ of the eye, would take the whole human being into its own

sphere, and not allow human beings to come to self-reliance. Human beings would only be able to see, they would not be able to think about what they had seen. They would be unable to detach themselves from what they saw and say: "I see." They would be overpowered by sight, as it were, unless this effect of lead existed in the Cosmos. It is this activity of lead which makes it possible for human beings to be independent in themselves, which places them as an ego as regards receptivity to the outer world, which lives in them. These lead-forces first enter the etheric body of human beings, and from the etheric body they also impregnate the physical body, in a certain sense. Thereby human beings receive the capacity of memory; the power of memory."[102]

Such is the quality of Saturn that it saves an imprint of every encounter and every occurrence in life. Saturn stands for the ability to form body-free memories, thoughts, and ideas.

Where do we find these qualities of dying to imprint? In the bones we can find an endpoint of the movement, a stillness. Everything has frozen into space. It is a point of death, and at the same time also a point of becoming—because in the marrow of the bones we find the birthplace of new blood. "Die and become" takes place here. It is interesting that archaeologists can use bones to find out a lot about the living conditions of past cultures. Human history is engraved right down to the bones. You may feel heaviness in this topic; the mood of the soul is serious. But the third quality next to "die and become" might lift your spirits.

Let us take a look at an organ that clearly shows the forces of Saturn and lead: the spleen. The spleen, as a lymphatic organ, can provide defense cells when they are needed. So it forms an active border to our interior and shields it—as Saturn shields our solar system from the rest of the universe. The spleen also breaks down old, used cells, including blood cells. A certain spiritual warmth goes hand in hand with this process of degradation and dying, because it sets something free. From it arises the capacity for enthusiasm. Finally, we have a third quality that makes the heaviness of the theme bearable: enthusiasm!

We can find evidence of the spark of enthusiasm in lead as well. If you take a piece of dull, gray lead and slice through it, you might be surprised to find a brilliant, shining silver inside—a little spark of enthusiasm. However, after only a brief exposure to the air, it oxidizes and turns the familiar gray again. It's like a secret, happy to be finally revealed, but not happy to linger in the spotlight. In a similar way, enthusiasm is not meant to be a constant state, but rather a brief injection of something new into a situation. Its effectiveness is due in part to its unexpectedness and fleeting nature.

To summarize this briefly, Saturn and lead processes work in us. In the heaviness, the rigidity, we find the bones, the decomposition of the old blood, but also the memory of the past. In the warmth, the collection of impressions, we see the defense, the formation of red blood cells, and the possibility of being able to think detached from the body. These are the forces of becoming. And as the final and third quality, in the shininess of the freshly cut lead, we see enthusiasm. Enthusiasm reorients us toward our ideals. This ability leads from the past orientation of Saturn into a future, where these ideals can be converted into action. Ultimately, remembering also has a future-oriented quality.

So when we come to the time of Saturn in our life, when we have gotten older and feel the dismantling forces in the physical, then we can animate the past with the inner warmth and thereby truly generate building forces for the future, which, so to speak, lies behind Saturn, that is, it lies after life. The resulting enthusiasm might help to lighten something heavy that we have been carrying through our lives.

Working with Saturn Forces in Daily Life: Tradition, Innovation, and a Spark of Enthusiasm

Tradition is the passing on of customs, manners, or conventions. It is something that acts from the past into the present. As discussed, Saturn is the bearer of memory. These memories work through the passing on of a tradition. It can be very pleasant to keep traditions alive. It gives a feeling of togetherness. What traditions in your family are very dear to you?

The opposite of tradition is innovation. Grappling with necessity for change can mark the end of tradition. But must this be so? Is it not also true that the tradition began with an innovation and then proved valuable to continue or repeat? Isn't tradition, strictly speaking, the deathblow of innovation? What happens at the threshold where tradition and innovation meet? Courage and fear must look at each other face-to-face.

What is the value of a tradition? It is said that a tradition is not to keep the ashes, but to pass on the fire. Are there traditions in your life where the fire has gone out? What ingredients would it take to rekindle such a cold tradition? It takes courage and fear! Courage is a forward-looking energy that gives us the necessary focus, despite resistance and adversity. Fear arises at the same time because the future that will arise from the transformation is not yet visible. Fear is often viewed as an obstacle or hindrance, and courage is welcomed. But if we give fear the opportunity to be seen as a positive tool, then its strength unfolds. Fear slows us down and makes us more attentive. The senses are sharpened; it is like a countermovement to courage. So if we see fear as a messenger, then we become more receptive to the future.

What is the relationship between fear and courage in these threshold moments? When fear leads, there may be a tendency to freeze or withdraw into the familiar. On the other hand, resisting or avoiding fear can lead to folly! To cross the threshold, we need the courage to let the past die with a healthy dose of fear of what is to come.

When opposites meet there is always a third force that can connect the opposites and transform them into something higher. In this case, enthusiasm is the impulse that can elevate fear and courage and push us across the threshold. A good image of this process is an archer. He draws the arrow in the bow and maintains this tension. The tension creates a kind of warmth; it is the courage that is built up in the concentration. When the tension has been held long enough and the calm approaches the stillness, the moment of reckoning comes. The spark of enthusiasm flashes, and the possibility of releasing the tension and sending the arrow on its way has irrevocably come. Now fear comes in place of courage. Will the arrow reach its target? If the courage is too weak, the tension will not be held long enough and the arrow will not be released into the intended path. If fear gets out of hand, the arrow will probably not be sent on its journey, and the archer will lower his bow without having achieved anything. And if the enthusiasm spills over into childish impatience, then the bow is not drawn properly and the arrow just flies in front of your feet. Such is the artful balance between courage, fear, and the spark of enthusiasm that can rekindle a tradition.

Let's take a look at an example: For generations, turkey has been the heart of an American Thanksgiving meal. This is the tradition in many families. But these days, many more people are vegetarians or have concerns over animal welfare. They doubt the meaningfulness of eating turkey or question its collective cost. When their courage gets out of hand, they trumpet loudly how cruel it is to kill an animal just because it's tradition and who came up with this nonsense, anyway? But if the fears dominate, the vegetarians might stay quiet and try to eat around the turkey as discreetly as possible. However, if a balance can form between the opposites ahead of time, it could resolve the potential situation. For example, perhaps a few weeks before Thanksgiving the subject of vegetarianism comes up in a family conversation. In this context, there can be a discussion of the Thanksgiving turkey, with everything that is nice about family holidays and traditions, as well as the reasons to end the practice in the family. The reactions might turn out to be varied despite the balanced play of forces of courage and fear. Between *clearly no problem* and *it was always like that, and we will keep it that way,* anything is possible. With a spark of enthusiasm, humor can appear to break the ice and tear a crack in tradition where new light can shine through. The tradition of Thanksgiving can be maintained (perhaps in a slightly altered manner), but with an updated way of celebrating that better suits the times and the group. Time is of the essence in this process. Courage needs time, stillness, and inner preparation to be at the ready. How can you bring up the topic? What do you want to say, what is the exact message? Fear requires good timing of when to speak out. Are all the people in charge of the meal present? Is everyone listening? Enthusiasm needs the flexibility to raise the issue again at another time, or to play with humor by inviting other examples and giving space to the other arguments. It is for sure an act of art to rekindle the fire of a worn out tradition.

> Are there traditions in your life that need a pinch of innovation? Have you ever tried to change something like this and how have you failed? Can you see any reasons in the example why you might have been unsuccessful?

Break Down the Wall

On November 30, 1979, the concept album *The Wall* was released by the British rock band Pink Floyd. With about 33 million records sold, it became one of the most successful albums of all time. The foundation for this rock opera was laid by an incident that occurred at the last concert of their *Animals* tour in Montreal. Pink Floyd was playing in big stadiums for the first time, and guitarist and singer Roger Waters felt it was more of a burden. It seemed to him as if the large audience was a roaring monster. When a drunk man set off firecrackers in the first row of the concert, Waters lost his temper and spat in the man's face. Afterwards he was so shocked about his emotional outburst that the idea of building a wall between the band and the audience was born. This then became the stage concept for *The Wall.*

The building of (inner) and outer walls runs through the history of humanity like a golden thread. Walls were built to not let their own out or to not let the foreign in. Famous representatives of the wall culture are, for example, the main wall of ancient Babylon with a total length of 8 km (4.98 miles). Another work of gigantic dimensions is the Great Wall of China. Building began in the seventh century BC and continued until the sixteenth century. With the galactic length of

21,196 km (13,170 miles) in total, it is visible even from outer space. The Wailing Wall, which protected the Second Temple of Jerusalem in the West, is today the most visited place in Jerusalem. The Berlin Wall was a famous representative of modern times; for twenty-eight years it separated East and West Germany, before the people tore it down in 1989.

Looking back to the rock opera *The Wall*, a deeper theme of bricks and walls is visible. It tells the story of Pink, a successful rock musician. Pink grows up without his father (who was killed in action during World War II), and his mother is overprotective. (Today one would say she was a helicopter mother.) She wants her son to stay with her for all time, never leave her, and never love another woman. *"Mamma's gonna keep you right here under her wing, she won't let you fly, but she might let you sing . . . ooh babe of course, Mamma's gonna help build the wall."*[103] He then succeeds in becoming a rock star, and he gets married. But his touring life is excessive, and he cheats on his wife. Then one day when he calls his wife from America, another man answers the phone. She has also cheated. The third agonizing part in his biography is mentioned as his school years, which were dominated by the cruelty of his teachers. *"When we grew up and went to school, there were certain teachers who would hurt the children in any way they could. (Oof!) By pouring their derision upon anything we did and exposing every weakness however carefully hidden by the kids."*[104]

Pink then decides to build a definitive wall around himself or, rather, to continue building on the wall that his mother had erected to protect him. Once it is built, however, he despairs of the social seclusion. The attempt to tear down the wall fails miserably. *"But it was only fantasy, the wall was too high, as you can see. No matter how he tried, he could not break free, and the worms ate into his brain. . ."*[105] This was followed by his final fall into drugs. At the end of this dark period, he can no longer suppress his emotions and accuses himself of the crime of showing feelings. Three witnesses are called before the imaginary court: his overprotective mother, his ex-wife who disrespects him, and the sadistic teacher. They condemn him once again in the worst way! As punishment he is to tear down his wall completely. *"Since, my friend, you have revealed your deepest fear, I sentence you to be exposed better by your peers, tear down the wall!"*[106]

The story ends quite abruptly in the midst of the song "Outside the Wall" with a so-called cold ending. The final words are: *"Isn't it where . . ."*[107] So it remains open how the story of Pink ends. The final song is actually directed at humanity as well. Many people have social barriers: How can we meet them and invite them to reconnect? Where are we builders of our own wall, and where is one being built around us? When are we building walls around other people or ideas?

The times when borders had to be physically visible and immortalized in elaborate walls are over. The borders in today's time are drawn and held with treaties and alliances. First, equality and democracy are regulated by laws. Second, the economic realm is managed by contractual agreements and regulatory boundaries. And third, there is (or ought to be) freedom in the spiritual life—in education, science, culture, and religion. This concept of "Social Threefolding" was developed by Rudolf Steiner in 1919. Steiner was reacting against the one-sidedness and corruption that he saw in both capitalism and socialism, in favor of a more balanced system where these spheres operated in a more humane and cooperative way: An economic sphere grounded in fraternity, where individuals employed their talents in service to others; a political sphere grounded in equal rights and responsibilities; and a cultural sphere where individuals could freely express themselves.[108] These ideas were relevant a century ago, and they are finding a real resurgence in modern times.

But here, too, limitations are found everywhere, so that freedom in particular cannot fully develop. The limits in freedom are walls, which do not belong there. Ideally, we educate our children to become free and independent personalities, but in the example of Pink's mother, this freedom is curtailed by her own fears. In schools, the curriculum is given by the state. There is rarely an opening for one's own ideas or approaches to be incorporated. True freedom cannot be limited, but are there no boundaries in its realm? Well, there is one boundary that would actually make all other boundaries obsolete. If we would pay full respect to this one threshold, then we all would be free instantly! This border does not run between countries, parties, belief systems, or concepts but between humans—it is the recognition and acknowledgment of the free individual in the other. It is easier said than done, but we can start our thinking with a wise word by Novalis who said: "*Touch is connection and separation at the same time.*"[109] Perhaps the sweetest wall we can build is when we put our arms around a person in an embrace.

Epilogue

Back Down to Earth

The French astronaut Thomas Pesquet said of returning to Earth, "When you return, you never really feel good because you've spent six months adapting to the conditions in space. In a way, it's like you're not an Earthling anymore—your body has changed."[110]

That astronauts' bodies have changed is not surprising. Spending time in an altered state of gravity influences all of the body's systems in more or less subtle ways. It takes time to re-establish a sense of normalcy.

Even after a trip on Earth, one eventually returns to the place of departure. Your pockets are empty, yet you are richly filled with experiences. "Where were you? How was it? What did you experience? Did you try something new? Did everything go as planned?" A wave of questions breaks over you—understandably—but actually you still feel like silence. Even astronauts who attend a parade in their honor shortly after landing will then retire to be medically rebuilt and to recover out of view.

Perhaps parents recognize the phenomenon of when children come home from summer camp and react extremely annoyed to their parents' questions about how it was. Or even after a day at school, some kids don't like to talk about it. They usually succinctly say they don't know what they did.

But what is this emptiness, this aloneness, this speechlessness about? The traveler or the child needs to mark the last stages of the journey and finally close the circle, like the hero who returns home the same and yet not the same. What follows is the necessary process of digestion, comparable to digesting a good meal. And like the physical digestion, where everything is destroyed and disassembled in the dark interior into usable elements for the body, the last steps of a journey also happen in the unconscious. One must first be able to forget everything, to let it slide into the unconscious. Only then, with the recollection, is the journey complete. But in our time, forgetting to be able to remember is not a common way to deal with experiences. We no longer wait two or three weeks for the photos to be developed and eagerly open the envelope to bring the treasures of memory into the light of day. Today the pictures are available instantly, and one is almost immediately compelled to show everything. In this way, experiences remain stuck to the surface, whereas they can only gain depth and develop into true individual and biographically relevant insights through the workings of the unconscious.

But looking back on this book and the various journeys it has invited into one's own inner space, into one's own biography, we started with the idea of the Hummingbird Principle. The principle described the necessity of knowing one's individual strengths and learning to use them to tackle the big problems of our time, as well as the smaller problems of everyday life, out of an inner moral intuition. The Hummingbird Principle offered us a framework that enabled us to journey to the seven biographically relevant planets, their specific qualities, and their connection to the stories of your life. Wherever the readers feel a resonance with the subject, that's where they should delve. We hope that each chapter offers an invitation to unveil hidden powers or to work to gain clarity on important life questions. When you pick this book up again years from now, you will read it with different eyes and perhaps other chapters will become important. Thus, it is intended to grow with the reader and reveal the secrets at the right time. Each of these inner journeys follows the described principles of departure, experience, return, digestion, forgetting, and remembering.

As a final thought, we would like to advocate for the value of forgetting. For this purpose, we invite you, dear reader, to forget all the themes you worked with in this book and to trust that only with the ability to remember will your journey be completed. The memory gained will thus be settled on a higher truth than what is apparent at this juncture. The true reason of each journey is developed in the unknown and reappears only after a period of dormancy to unveil its precious secrets.

Acknowledgments

Like any good project, writing this book has been a journey. The preparations for the journey began in our Biography and Social Art training when we paired up for an assignment, which asked us to develop and offer a public workshop. After hashing out the details of our workshop, we ambitiously set up two dates to offer it. Exactly one person showed up for the first date. We thought about canceling, but then here was this one person who wanted to hear what we had to say. So we chose to ride the wave (Mercury, see chapter 2). We went through the whole workshop, participating in every exercise ourselves, and it was great—not perfect, but complete (Jupiter, see chapter 6). We told the lone participant that when we wrote our book, we would show her our gratitude by saying, "It all started with April in November." That was when the journey began in earnest.

The journey has been long, and it has had its share of ups and downs. We are grateful to each other for remaining committed to the project in the face of challenges and setbacks (Mars, see chapter 5). We have learned and grown from these experiences, and we wonder (Moon, see chapter 1) what their significance will be in the long run. Thanks to Linda Roghaar at White River Press for believing in our vision and practicing patience while we and our ideas matured (Venus, see chapter 3), and to our editor Jean Stone for helping to sharpen our language and make everything more readable. We had to be courageous enough to let some ideas die so that clearer and better ones could come through (Saturn, see chapter 7), and the book is stronger because of her input. And finally, thanks to all of our friends and relations who have been a part of this journey and given us so many gifts along the way (Sun, see chapter 4). They've been our teachers, they've connected us to the right people at the right time, they've offered both supportive and challenging feedback, they've given us a platform for our work, they've asked (repeatedly) how the book is coming along, and they've shown up for our lectures and workshops. Chris would especially like to thank his wife Jerilyn for her ongoing love and support throughout this process despite the challenges it created for her. If we become who we surround ourselves with, we might just turn out okay.

About the Authors

CHRIS BURKE WAS BORN AND RAISED IN PENNSYLVANIA, US. HE EARNED a PhD in social psychology from New York University and is an associate professor of psychology at Lehigh University, where his research has focused on social relationships and coping with stress. He teaches courses on topics ranging from grief and anxiety to how to live a meaningful life, always bringing biographical assignments to help students connect the content to their own experiences. He lives with his wife Jerilyn and three amazing children along the Delaware River in eastern Pennsylvania.

ANNE DE WILD WAS BORN IN ROTTERDAM, THE NETHERLANDS, AND moved to Switzerland at the age of three. She is certified as a Traditional European Naturopath (TEN) and runs a private practice in Basel. Her training in biography work is crucial to working with clients, creating a personal connection between the issue at hand and the individual's life story. In addition, she offers lectures and workshops on various topics, including the five temperaments and the phases of life. She is the mother of three daughters and a son and is slowly stepping into the role of grandmother.

For more information about Chris and Anne's work, including access to online courses and essays, visit their website at www.thehummingbirdprinciple.com.

Notes

Introduction

1   Rudolf Steiner, *Anthroposophical Leading Thoughts*, trans. G. Adams & M. Adams (London: Rudolf Steiner Press, 1973), 13.

2   Steiner, "Awakening to Community" (lecture IV, Stuttgart, Germany, Feb. 13, 1923), accessed Aug. 22, 2022, https://rsarchive .org/Lectures/CW257/English/AP1974/19230213p02.html.

3   Steiner, "The Younger Generation" (lecture VI, Stuttgart, Germany, Oct. 8, 1922), https://rsarchive.org/Lectures/CW217/English/ AP1967/.

4   Note that all Rudolf Steiner quotes in this book have been adapted for gender neutrality from the original masculine form.

5   Steiner, "The Younger Generation" (lecture I, Stuttgart, Germany, Oct. 3, 1922), CW 217.

6   Martin Heidegger, *Being and Time* (Tübingen, Germany: Max Niemeyer Verlag, 1953; Albany, NY: State University of New York Press, 1996).

7   Rainer Maria Rilke, *Letters to a Young Poet* (London: Penguin Random House, 2016).

8   Michael Nicoll Yahgulanaas, *The Little Hummingbird* (Vancouver, BC, Canada: Greystone Books, 2010).

9   Steiner, *Intuitive Thinking as a Spiritual Path: A Philosophy of Freedom*, ch. 9 (1894; Hudson, NY: Anthroposophic Press, 1995).

10   Steiner, *Theosophy* (Hudson, NY: Anthroposophic Press, 1994). See also E. F. Schumacher, *A Guide for the Perplexed* (New York: Harper & Row, 1977).

11   Steiner, "The Apocalypse of St. John" (lecture VIII, Nuremberg, Germany, June 25, 1908), CW 104.

12   M. K. Rothbart, D. Derryberry, & K. Hershey, "Stability of Temperament in Childhood: Laboratory Infant Assessment to Parent Report at Seven Years," *Temperament and Personality Development Across the Life Span*, eds. V. J. Molfese, D. L. Molfese, & R. R. McCrae (New York: Psychology Press, 2000), 85–119.

Chapter 1 – MOON

13   R. A. Wicklund & Gollwitzer, *Symbolic Self-Completion* (New York: Routledge, 1982).

14   C. G. Jung, "Concerning Rebirth," *The Collected Works of C. G. Jung*, vol. 9, pt. 1; *Archetypes and the Collective Unconscious*, ed. Gerhard Adler and R. F. C. Hull (Princeton, NJ: Princeton

University Press, 1969), 111-148, http://www.jstor.org/stable /j.ctt5hhrnk.10.

15   Jung, "Concerning Rebirth," . . . , 123.

16   R. A. Johnson, *Owning Your Own Shadow: Understanding the Dark Side of the Psyche* (New York: HarperCollins, 1991).

17   Johnson, *Owning Your Own Shadow* . . . , 7–8.

18   A. Adler, *Understanding Human Nature* (London: George Allen & Unwin Ltd., 1923).

19   D. Bassok, S. Latham, & A. Rorem, "Is Kindergarten the New First Grade?" *AERA Open* 1, no. 4 (2016): 1–31.

20   P. Gray, "The Decline of Play and the Rise of Psychopathology in Children and Adolescents," *American Journal of Play* 3, no. 4 (2011): 443–463.

21   K. Durkin, M. W. Lipsey, D. C. Farran, & S. E. Wiesen, "Effects of a Statewide Pre-Kindergarten Program on Children's Achievement and Behavior through Sixth Grade," *Developmental Psychology* 58, no. 3, (2022): 470–484.

22   J. Korczak, *How to Love a Child and Other Selected Works*, vol. 1 (Elstree, UK: Vallentine Mitchell, 2018).

23   W. Szpilman, *The Pianist* (New York: Picador USA, 1999), 95–96.

24   J. Korczak, *How to Love a Child* . . . , 123, accessed Aug. 11, 2022, http://www.januszkorczak.ca/legacy/3_How%20to%20Love%20 a%20Child.pdf.

Chapter 2 – MERCURY

25   K. Robinson, "Do Schools Kill Creativity?" (lecture, TED Talk, 2006), accessed Aug. 11, 2022, https://www.ted.com/talks/sir_ ken_robinson_do_schools_kill_creativity.

26   H. Prather, *Notes to Myself: My Struggle to Become a Person* (New York: Bantam Books, 1970).

27   C. R. Rogers, "A Theory of Therapy, Personality, and Interpersonal Relationships: As Developed in the Client-Centered Framework," S. Koch, ed. *Psychology: A Study of a Science. Formulations of the Person and the Social Context*, vol. 3 (New York: McGraw Hill, 1959), 184–256.

28   C. R. Rogers, "Toward a Theory of Creativity," *ETC: A Review of General Semantics* 11, no. 4 (1954): 249–260.

29   *Inspirations*, directed by Michael Apted, interviews with David Bowie, Roy Lichtenstein, Dale Chihuly, Édouard Lock, Louise LeCavalier, Nora Naranjo-Morse, & Tadao Ando (Argo Films, 1997).

30   N. Copernicus, *On the Revolutions of the Heavenly Spheres*, trans. C. G. Wallis (1543; Amherst, NY: Prometheus Books, 1995), 292.

31   K. König, *The Human Soul* (Hudson, NY: Anthroposophic Press, 1973), 22.

32   K. König, *The Human Soul*, 21.

33   S. K. Scott, N. Lavan, S. Chen, & C. McGettigan, "The Social Life of Laughter," *Trends in Cognitive Sciences* 18, no. 12 (2014): 618–620, https://doi.org/10.1016/j.tics.2014.09.002.

Chapter 3 — VENUS

34   V. Flusser, *Von der Freiheit des Migranten*, trans. A. de Wild (Hamburg, Germany: CEP Europäische Verlagsanstalt, 2013), 11.

35   Flusser, *Von der Freiheit des Migranten*, 13.

36   Emily Dickinson, "I died for Beauty, but was scarce . . . ," c. 1862, https://www.edickinson.org/editions/2/image_sets/12170088.

37   S. Rossi, "Libra, Aphrodite, and the Horai," *The Archetypal Eye*, Oct. 16, 2016, accessed Aug. 9, 2022, https://www.thearchetypaleye.com/blog/2016/10/15/libra-aphrodite-and-the-horai.

38   Ovid, *Metamorphoses*, Book III, trans. Sir Samuel Garth, John Dryden, et al, accessed Aug. 10, 2022, http://classics.mit.edu/Ovid/metam.3.third.html.

39   Jacob and Wilhelm Grimm, *Children's and Household Tales*, final edition (Berlin: 1857), no. 53, Snow-White.

40   See also H. Schramm, *The Healing Power of Planetary Metals in Anthroposophic and Homeopathic Medicine* (Great Barrington, MA: Lindisfarne Books, 2013).

41   Eugen Drewermann, *Landschaften der Seele oder: Wie wir Mann und Frau werden* (Patmos: 2015), 3–172.

42   G. Bateson, D. D. Jackson, J. Haley, & J. Weakland, "Toward a theory of schizophrenia," *Behavioral Science*, vol. 1 (1956): 251–264.

43   M. B. Brewer, "Optimal Distinctiveness Theory: Its History and Development," *Handbook of Theories of Social Psychology* (London: Sage Publications, 2012): 81–98.

44   For a summary, see C. Holdrege, "Goethe and the Evolution of Science," *In Context*, 31 (Spring 2014): 10–23.

45   P. J. Palmer, *To Know as We Are Known: A Spirituality of Education* (San Francisco, CA: Harper & Row, 1983).

46   A. Frank, *The Diary of a Young Girl* (New York: Bantam Books, 1952), 542.

Chapter 4 — SUN

47   T. Gioia, *Love Songs: The Hidden History* (Oxford, UK: Oxford University Press, 2015).

48   S. A. Mehr, M. Singh, H. York, L. Glowacki, & M. M. Krasnow, "Form and Function in Human Song," *Current Biology* 28 (2018): 356–368.

49   W. Shakespeare, *The Merry Wives of Windsor* (1602: London: Cassell & Company Ltd., 1888), 2.2.2–3.

50   C. G. Jung, *Modern Man in Search of a Soul* (London: Kegan Paul, Trench, Trubner & Co Ltd., 1933), 124.

51   C. G. Jung, M.-L.von Franz, J. L. Henderson, J. Jacobi, & A. Jaffé, *Man and His Symbols* (New York: Anchor Press, 1964), 212.

52   A. Ransome, *The Fool of the World and the Flying Ship* (New York: Farrar, Straus and Giroux, 1968).

53   F. Sakade & Y. Kurosaki, *Little One-Inch and Other Japanese Children's Favorite Stories* (Clarendon, VT: Tuttle Publishing, 2008).

54   P. Coelho, *The Alchemist* (New York: HarperCollins, 1993), 22.

55   Michael Anthony, David Lee Roth, Eddie Van Halen, Alex Van Halen, "Runnin' with the Devil" (1978).

56   L. Nummenmaa, E. Glerean, R. Hari, & J. K. Hietanen, "Bodily Map of Emotions," *Proceedings of the National Academy of Sciences* 111, no. 2 (2014): 646–651.

57   J. L. Tracy & D. Randles, "Four Models of Basic Emotions: A Review of Ekman and Cordaro, Izard, Levenson, and Panksepp and Watt," *Emotion Review* 3, no. 4 (2011): 397–405.

58   P. Ekman & D. Cordaro, "What is Meant by Calling Emotions Basic," *Emotion Review* 3, no. 4 (2011): 364–370.

59   C. D. Hayden, "Remembering John Lewis: The Power of 'Good Trouble,'" *Timeless: Stories from the Library of Congress* (July 19, 2020), accessed July 19, 2023, https://blogs.loc.gov/loc/2020/07/remembering-john-lewis-the-power-of-good-trouble/.

60 Matt. 21:12–13 (NKJV).

61 Steiner, *Metamorphoses of the Soul* I (lecture II, "The Mission of Anger," Berlin, Germany, Dec. 5, 1909), CW 58.

62 R. B. Cialdini, B. L. Darby, & J. E. Vincent, "Transgression and Altruism: A Case for Hedonism," *Journal of Experimental Social Psychology* 9 (1973): 502–516.

63 E. Walster, E. Berscheid, & G. W. Walster, "New Directions in Equity Research," *Journal of Personality and Social Psychology* 25, no. 2 (1973): 151–176.

64 M. S. Clark, J. Mills, & M. C. Powell, "Keeping Track of Needs in Communal and Exchange Relationships," *Journal of Personality and Social Psychology* 51, no. 2 (1986): 333–338.

65 M. E. J. Gleason. M. Iida, N. Bolger, & P. E. Shrout, "Daily Supportive Equity in Close Relationships," *Personality and Social Psychology Bulletin* 29, no. 8 (2003): 1036–1045.

66 C. T. Burke & J. Goren, "Self-Evaluative Consequences of Social Support Receipt: The Role of Context Self-Relevance," *Personal Relationships* 21 (2014): 433–450.

67 R. B. Cialdini, R. J. Borden, A. Thorne, M. R. Walker, S. Freeman, & L. R. Sloan, "Basking in Reflected Glory: Three (Football) Field Studies," *Journal of Personality and Social Psychology* 3 (1976): 366–375.

68 A. Tesser, "Toward a Self-Evaluation Maintenance Model of Social Behavior," R. F. Baumeister, ed. *Advances in Experimental Social Psychology*, vol. 21 (Cambridge, MA: Academic Press, 1988), 181–227.

69 S. Brotbeck, *Zukunft: Aspekte eines Rätsels* (Dornach, Switzerland: Verlag am Goetheanum, 2005).

Chapter 5 — MARS

70 W. von Eschenbach, *Parzival: A Romance of the Middle Ages,* trans. H. M. Mustard & C. E. Passage (New York: Vintage Books, 1961).

71 B. Lievegoed, *Phases: The Spiritual Rhythms in Adult Life* (Forest Row, UK: Sophia Books, 1997), 69.

72 S. Reiss, *Who Am I? The 16 Basic Desires That Motivate Our Actions and Define Our Personalities* (New York: Berkley Books, 2000).

73 V. E. Frankl, (1947/1984). *Man's Search for Meaning,* 3rd ed. (1947; New York: Simon & Schuster, 1984.)

74 V. E. Frankl, *Man's Search for Meaning,* 74.

75 J. Nazar, *10 Lessons Entrepreneurs Can Learn from Superheroes* (2008), accessed May 30, 2023, https://youtu.be/fBGT8TVjZXQ.

76 John Donne, *Devotions Upon Emergent Occasions, and Several Steps in My Sickness* (London: Thomas Jones, 1624), 415–416.

77 H. Selye, *The Stress of Life* (New York: McGraw Hill, 1956).

78 Steiner, *How to Know Higher Worlds,* trans. C. Bamford (1904; Hudson, NY: Anthroposophic Press, 1994), 101–102.

79 Wolfgang Held, *Rhythms of the Week: And Other Explorations of Time* (Edinburgh, UK: Floris Books, 2011) 42.

80 Vilém Flusser, *Von der Freiheit des Migranten* (EVA Taschenbuch), trans. A. de Wild (2013), 13.

Chapter 6 — JUPITER

81 Richard Rohr, *Falling Upward: A Spirituality for the Two Halves of Life* (San Francisco, CA: Jossey-Bass, 2011).

82 Rohr, *Falling Upward: . . .*

83 E. M. Cybulska, "Boléro unravelled: A case of musical perseveration," *Psychiatric Bulletin* 21 (1997): 576–577.

84 W. W. Seeley, B. R. Matthews, R. K. Crawford, M. L. Gorno-Tempini, D. Foti, I. R. Mackenzie, & B. L. Miller, "Unravelling Boléro: Progressive aphasia, transmodal creativity and the right posterior neocortex," *Brain* 131, no. 1 (2008): 39–49.

85 Roberto Assagioli, *The Balancing and Synthesis of the Opposites,* vol. 29 (New York, NY: Psychosynthesis Research Foundation, 1972), 2–8.

86 Assagioli, *The Balancing and Synthesis . . .*

87 M. R. Leary & R. F. Baumeister, "The Nature and Function of Self-Esteem: Sociometer Theory," M. P. Zanna, ed., *Advances in Experimental Social Psychology*, vol. 32 (San Diego, CA: Academic Press, 2000), 1–62.

88 C. R. Rogers, "A Theory of Therapy, Personality, and Interpersonal Relationships: As Developed in the Client-Centered Framework," S. Koch, ed., *Psychology: A Study of a Science. Formulations of the Person and the Social Context*, vol. 3 (New York: McGraw Hill, 1959), 184–256.

89 E. Fromm, *Escape from Freedom* (New York: Macmillan, 1994).

90 E. Fromm, *Escape from Freedom.*

91 J.-P. Sartre, *Being and Nothingness*, trans. H. Barnes (1943; New York: Philosophical Library, 1956).

92 From the song "Freewill" by Rush, vocals by Geddy Lee, lyrics by Neil Peart (1980).

93 Steiner, "The Spiritual Individualities of the Planets" (lecture 1, Dornach, Switzerland, July 27, 1923), CW 228.

94   S. Winchester, *The Professor and the Madman* (New York: Harper Perennial, 2005).

95   M. Chabon, *Wonder Boys* (New York: Random House, 1995).

Chapter 7 — SATURN

96   S. Brotbeck, *Zukunft: Aspekte eines Rätsels* (Dornach, Switzerland: Verlag am Goetheanum, 2005).

97   R. Kreibich, B. Oertel, & M. Wolk, "Futures Studies and Future-Oriented Technology Analysis Principles, Methodology, and Research Questions," *HIIG Discussion Paper Series No. 2012–05* (2012), http://dx.doi.org/10.2139/ssrn.2094215.

98   From the song "Unanswered Prayers" by Garth Brooks, lyrics by Pat Alger, Larry Bastian, and Garth Brooks (1990).

99   https://www.etymonline.com/word/regret.

100   T. Gilovich & V. H. Medvec, "The Experience of Regret: What, When, and Why," *Psychological Review* 102, no. 2 (1995): 379–395.

101   G. Coricelli, R. J. Dolan, & A. Sirigu, "Brain, Emotion, and Decision Making: The Paradigmatic Example of Regret," *Trends in Cognitive Science* 11, no. 6 (2007): 258–265.

102   Steiner, "Mystery Centres," *The Chthonic and the Eleusinian Mysteries* (lecture X: Dornach, Switzerland, Dec. 14, 1923), CW 232.

103   Pink Floyd, Pink, Lyrics from the song "Mamma," *The Wall* (1979).

104   Pink Floyd, Lyrics from the song "The Happiest Days of Our Lives," *The Wall*.

105   Pink Floyd, Lyrics from the song "Hey You," *The Wall*.

106   Pink Floyd, Lyrics from the song "Trial," *The Wall*.

107   Pink Floyd, Lyrics from the song "Outside the Wall," *The Wall*.

108 Steiner, *The Threefold Social Order*, trans. F. C. Heckel (1919; New York: Anthroposophic Press, 1972).

109 Novalis, *Notes for a Romantic Encyclopaedia, Das Allgemeine Brouillon*, trans. & ed. David W. Wood, 1st group: para. 295, "Cosmologie" (1798/1799; Albany, NY: State University of New York Press, 2007 ed.).

Epilogue

110 A. Koehler, "Back Down to Earth: An Astronaut's Perspective," *European Space Agency blog*, accessed May 30, 2023, https://blogs.esa.int/alexander-gerst/2018/12/13/back-to-earth-astronaut-perspective/.